THE FOLIO BOOK OF
CARD GAMES

THE FOLIO BOOK OF CARD GAMES

A Compendium of
Rare and *Remarkable* Games
of *Skill* and *Chance*

SELECTED FROM HOYLE'S RULES

WITH DECORATIONS BY
Clare Mackie

LONDON
The Folio Society
2009

The Folio Book of Card Games is selected from *Hoyle's Rules of Games: Descriptions of Indoor Games of Skill and Chance, with advice on Skillful Play. Based on the Foundations Laid Down by Edmond Hoyle, 1672–1769.* This selection is taken from the third edition by Albert H. Morehead and Geoffrey Mott-Smith (eds), and revised and updated by Philip D. Morehead, published by NAL Signet in 2001.

Published by arrangement with NAL Signet, a member of Penguin Group (USA) Inc.

SET IN BELL AT THE FOLIO SOCIETY.
PRINTED AT HIMMER AG, AUGSBURG, GERMANY. BOUND BY
LACHENMAIER, REUTLINGEN, GERMANY, PRINTED WITH A
DESIGN BY THE ARTIST

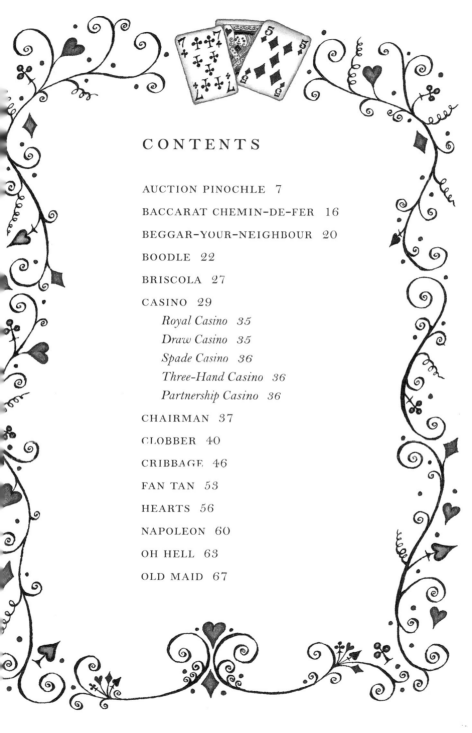

CONTENTS

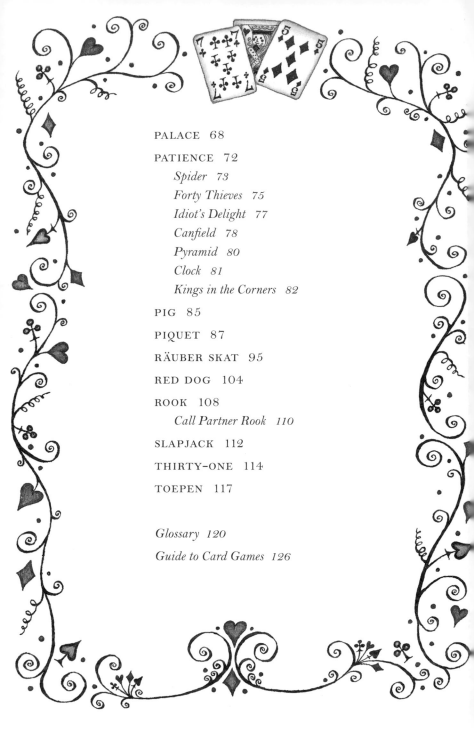

AUCTION PINOCHLE

Pinochle *is the name of a whole family of games, related by origin and having certain basic features in common, but varying widely in form and strategy. The two-hand game is almost identical with the French game* Bézique. *It was developed in the United States probably in the middle of the nineteenth century. The whole family grew up in the United States – not in Germany, as many persons assume merely because Pinochle games use a German ranking of the cards and took some of their features from German games such as Skat.*

Auction Pinochle is one of the best three-hand card games in history (in opportunities for skill) and was once among the most popular forms of Pinochle. It has since lost out to Bridge and to various forms of Rummy.

PLAYERS. Though only three are active at a time, the game is best for four; and five may sit at the table and participate. With four, dealer gives himself no cards.

With five, he omits himself and the second player to his left.

CARDS. The Pinochle pack is 48 cards, using two packs of 24 cards, made by taking out any cards less than 9 and shuffling together to use as one pack.

RANK OF CARDS. In each suit the rank is: A (high), 10, K, Q, J, 9. When duplicates are played to the same trick (as two aces of spades) the first-played ranks as higher.

CARD VALUES. The higher cards have the following scoring values when won in tricks:

	ORIGINAL COUNT	SIMPLIFIED COUNT
Each ace	11	10
Each ten	10	10
Each king	4	5
Each queen	3	5
Each jack	2	0

(No count for lower cards.)

Winning the last trick usually counts as 10 points. Under either the original or the simplified count, the total points at stake in the play are thus 250.

MELDS. Certain combinations of cards (melds) have the following scoring values.

SEQUENCES

A–K–Q–J–10 of trumps (flush)	150
K–Q of trumps (royal marriage)	40
K–Q of any other suit (simple marriage)	20

8

♠A-♥A-♦A-♣A (hundred aces)	100
♠K-♥K-♦K-♣K (eighty kings)	80
♠Q-♥Q-♦Q-♣Q (sixty queens)	60
♠J-♥J-♦J-♣J (forty jacks)	40

SPECIAL

♠Q-♦J (pinochle)	40
9 of trumps (dix, pronounced 'deece')	10

A card may be used in two or three melds, provided that they are of different classes. For example, the same ♠Q may be used in a marriage, sixty queens and pinochle. But when a flush is melded, the K-Q do not count separately as a royal marriage.

THE DEAL. Each player receives fifteen cards, dealt in batches. Dealer is usually allowed to follow his own preference among many plans: three at a time, or 4-4-4-3, etc. But he must adhere to the plan he commences. After the first round of the deal, three cards are dealt face down on the table, forming the *widow*.

BIDDING. Each player in turn to the left of the dealer must make a bid or pass. A player may continue bidding in turn in effort to win the contract, but once he has passed he is out of the bidding.

Each bid is a number of points, a multiple of ten. No suit is mentioned. It is customary to require the player to the left of the dealer to open with a compulsory bid; the minimum is usually set at 300, but it is 250 or 200 in various circles. No other player need bid if he prefers to pass.

The highest bidder becomes the *Bidder*. The other two become *Opponents*, combining in temporary partnership against him.

THE WIDOW. The Bidder turns the widow face up for all to see. He may then take the cards into his hand. Next he may meld; no other player may do so.

MELDING. The Bidder may put face up on the table all his cards that form proper melds (see pp. 8–9). The value of all such melds is totalled as the first item in his (potential) score. A roundhouse (K-Q in every suit) is scored as 240.

The Bidder may change his melds and the trump suit at any time before he has made the opening lead.

CONCESSION. The Bidder may concede defeat before leading. In this event, he loses *single bete* (pronounced 'bate'). Or, the Opponents may concede that he will surely make his bid, and then there is no play. One Opponent's concession is not binding on the other.

If the Bidder's melds total as much as, or more than, his bid, his contract is scored as made and there is no play. (The Bidder need not win a trick to count his melds.)

BURYING. If the Bidder needs some points from play to make his bid, and if he elects to play, he buries (discards) any three cards from his hand face down. He must not bury any card he has used in a meld, but he may bury trumps and aces. The buried cards belong to the Bidder after the play, and he counts them along with his tricks. After burying, the Bidder picks up all his melds. He names the trump suit (if he has not already indicated it by melding a flush or by claiming forty for a royal marriage).

10

THE PLAY. The Bidder makes the opening lead. He may lead any card, not necessarily a trump. The hands are played out in tricks. A player must follow suit to a lead, if able. If unable to follow to a nontrump lead, he must trump, if able. When a trump is led, he must play higher than any card already in the trick, if able. (He need not overtrump a trump previously played on a nontrump lead.) A trick is won by the highest trump in it, or, if it contains no trump, by the highest card played of the suit led. The winner of a trick leads to the next.

Tricks won by the Opponents are gathered in one pile.

RESULT OF PLAY. The Bidder examines his tricks and buried cards, and totals his count for high cards won. He also scores ten for last trick, if he wins it. If his count for cards plus his melds equals or surpasses his bid, the bid is made; if his total is less, the bid is defeated – or, as is said, the Bidder goes *double bete*.

SCORING. Though score can be kept on paper, the prevalent method is to settle with poker chips after each deal.

The payments are based on a schedule that varies with the locality; the most common is as follows:

BID	BASE VALUE
300 to 340	1
350 to 390	2
400 to 440	4
450 to 490	7
500 to 540	10
550 to 590	13

11

The base value is doubled when spades are trumps.

(A bid as high as 600 is hardly possible; bids over 450 are extremely rare.)

When the Bidder concedes single bete, he pays the base value of his bid to each Opponent. When he suffers double bete, he pays each Opponent (including inactive ones) twice the base value – four times if in spades. When the bid is made, the Bidder collects its base value (doubled in spades) from each Opponent.

THE KITTY. It is usual to maintain a kitty, a common pool of chips. When a player makes a forced opening bid (300, 250 or 200) and concedes single bete without looking at the widow, he pays the base value of his bid only to the kitty. In other cases the kitty neither pays nor collects on bids up to 340. On bids of 350 or more, the kitty collects and pays just as though it were a player.

The kitty is originally formed, and is replenished if necessary, by equal contributions and is divided equally among the players when a session ends.

Irregularities in Auction Pinochle

NEW DEAL. There must be a new deal by the same dealer if any card of the widow is exposed in dealing, or any two cards in players' hands; or if the pack was not properly shuffled and cut and attention is called to the fact before the widow is dealt.

EXPOSURE OF WIDOW. If, before the bidding ends, a player sees a card in the widow, he may not make another bid. If he exposes a card in the widow, there must be a new deal by the next dealer, and the offender must pay to each other player (including the kitty and inactive players) the base value of the highest bid made prior to his offence.

WRONG NUMBER OF CARDS. If a player has too few cards and another player or the widow has too many: (a) if the error is discovered before the Bidder has properly exposed the widow, the incorrect hands must be rectified; (b) if it is discovered at any later time, the bid is made if Bidder's hand (and discard, if any) are correct; if it is incorrect, the Bidder loses single or double bete, according to whether he has led.

If the widow is found to have too few cards, there must be another deal by the same dealer.

EXPOSED CARDS. The Bidder is not subject to penalty for exposing cards. If a player exposes one card during the bidding and then becomes an Opponent, the Bidder may require or forbid the lead or play of that card at the offender's first opportunity to play it. If the Opponents expose two or more cards after the opening lead, the bid is made.

BID OUT OF TURN. A bid out of turn is void without penalty, but it may be accepted as regular by the one or two other players still entitled to bid.

IMPROPER BURYING. If, after the Bidder leads, he is found to have buried a card he melded, or to have buried too many cards, he is double bete.

RENEGE. A player reneges if he fails, when able, to follow suit to a lead, play over on a trump lead, trump a plain lead or play an exposed card as properly required by the Bidder. The Bidder may correct a renege without penalty before he has played to the next trick. An Opponent may correct a renege before he or his partner has played to the next trick, but if the Bidder does not make his bid, the deal is void. Cards played after a renege may be withdrawn if it is corrected.

If a renege is not corrected in time, play ends forthwith. If the offender was an Opponent, the bid is made; if it was the Bidder, he is double bete.

LEAD OUT OF TURN. If the Bidder leads out of turn, there is no penalty but the correct leader may accept it or require it to be withdrawn. If an Opponent leads out of turn, the offence is treated as a renege.

ERROR IN COUNT OF MELD. If an incorrect value was agreed upon for the Bidder's meld, correction may be made at any time before settlement is completed.

Strategy of Auction Pinochle

In bidding, you may properly expect the widow to improve the playing value of your hand by twenty, but do not expect it to fill a needed meld unless you have at least five 'places open' (any of five outstanding cards will fill). As Bidder, play the hand rather than concede unless the odds are 2−1 or worse against making. (When spades count double, play a doubtful spade hand if the chances are not worse than even against you.)

In burying, usually discard a weak short holding (three cards or less with no ace). Save your longest side suit entire. Sometimes you may well bury one or two 10s, to save them from falling to the Opponents.

The commonest type of hand that you are forced to play as Bidder contains a trump suit of five or more cards, not solid, with a side suit of four or more. After cashing blank aces, if any, open the side suit and continue it at every opportunity. You may eventually force an Opponent to trump, thereby weakening his trump stoppers, and if this is a trick his partner would have won anyhow with a high card, you have escaped a *smear* (or *schmier*). The novice's most frequent error is leading trumps.

As an Opponent, usually try to force the Bidder to trump a plain suit. But sometimes, and especially when the Bidder needs few points, a better plan is to lead trumps. Unless there is a suit with which the Opponents can force the Bidder to trump, they should try to have the trick won by the Opponent who can lead through the Bidder.

The most costly error is bidding on hope rather than cards actually held. The chances of finding a specific card in the widow are:

PLACES OPEN	APPROXIMATE ODDS
1	5–1 against
2	2–1 against
3	Even
4	3–2 for
5	2–1 for

Baccarat, *a game related in principle to Blackjack, which is so popular in the United States, is the principal gambling card game of France and several other European countries. In recent years the original game of Baccarat has been all but replaced by this speeded-up version.*

PLAYERS. In a Baccarat Chemin-de-Fer game there are usually ten or more players, and almost any number can play, for it is a banking game. Every player has a chance to be banker.

CARDS. Several regular 52-card packs are shuffled together, usually at least three packs. The players take portions of the packs and shuffle them, trading them around to mix them thoroughly. The packs finally are placed in a device called a 'shoe', from which the cards can be slid out one by one.

BETTING. There is an auction to determine the first banker, who is the one willing to bid the largest sum to be his 'bank'. The banker then deals three or four cards from the shoe, showing them as he does so, and tossing them into a tray reserved for discards. The game is ready to begin.

Any player may make any bet, up to the amount of the bank, that the banker will lose. The player at the banker's right has the first chance to bet; any part of the bank he does not take may be bet by the player at his right; and so on in order to the right until the entire bank is covered or until everyone has bet who wishes to. Any player may take the entire bank by saying 'Banco', but when two or more players wish to banco the one nearest the banker's right has the privilege.

The banker is never liable for the payment of bets in excess of his bank.

THE PLAY. Bets being placed, the banker deals two hands of two cards each, dealing one card at a time. The hand he deals first represents all the players betting against him; the other hand is the banker's. The player who made the largest bet against the banker plays the opposition hand; and again, if there is a question of precedence, it goes to the player nearest the banker's right.

The object of the game is to hold two or three cards which count 9, or as nearly 9 as possible. The values of the cards are: face cards and tens, 0; aces, 1 each; any other card, its number. Units of 10 points are disregarded, so that 9 + 7 count as 6, not 16.

A player whose count is 9 or 8 in his first two cards shows his hand immediately. He has a natural and his

17

hand wins (but a natural 9 beats a natural 8). Naturals of the same number tie, and there is a new deal.

When the result is not decided by a natural, the banker must 'give' (a card) to his opponent on request; or the opponent may stand. The opponent *must* stand on 6 or 7, *must* draw to 4, 3, 2, 1, or 0, but has the option on 5. The additional card, if given, is face up.

Now the banker decides whether to stand or take a card. The following table shows the guidelines usually employed:

IF BANKER GIVES	BANKER STANDS ON	BANKER DRAWS TO
Face card or ten	4, 5, 6, 7	3, 2, 1, 0
Nine	4, 5, 6, 7 (or 3)	2, 1, 0 (or 3)
Eight	3, 4, 5, 6, 7	2, 1, 0
Seven or six	7	6, 5, 4, 3, 2, 1, 0
Five or four	6, 7	5, 4, 3, 2, 1, 0
Three or two	5, 6, 7	4, 3, 2, 1, 0
Ace	4, 5, 6, 7	3, 2, 1, 0
Opponent stands	6, 7	5, 4, 3, 2, 1, 0

Neither player may have more than one additional card, giving him three cards at most. When each has exercised his option, the cards are shown. If the totals are the same, the bets are off and may be withdrawn, and new bets are placed, exactly as before, for another deal. If the opponent has a higher number than the banker's, each player collects such portion of the bank as he covered, and the player to the banker's right becomes the next banker, naming any amount as his bank (there is no further auction). If the banker has the higher total, he collects all bets and remains the banker; the original bank plus the winnings remain as the new bank, and bets are placed as explained before.

No player is forced to be or remain the banker. The banker may always retire and pass the bank along, and any player in turn may take it or refuse it. But until he passes the bank, the banker may not remove from it any part of his winnings.

BEGGAR-YOUR-
NEIGHBOUR

Beggar-Your-Neighbour *is a time-tested children's favourite that is enjoyably undemanding for adults and sometimes goes by the bizarre name Strip-Jack-Naked.*

This game depends entirely on the luck of the shuffle. Two play. Each player receives half of the pack, face down. Nondealer turns up a card from the top of his packet and places it on the table. Dealer then turns up a card from his packet and places it upon the other. Play continues in the same way until the appearance of a face card or ace.

When one player turns up a high card, the other must place upon it: four cards for an ace, three for a king, two for a queen, one for a jack. If the high card draws its quota in lower cards (ten or lower), the player of the high card takes up the entire common pile, places it face down under his packet, and leads for a new series of plays. But if a face card or ace appears in the course of playing the quota on an opponent's high card, the obligation is reversed, and the opponent must give a quota. This alternation continues until a player wins the pile.

The player who gets the entire pack into his hands wins the game. This may happen in one 'run-through' or the game may continue for a long time.

BOODLE

Boodle *is the best-known member of the* Stops *family, in which a player's turn can be stopped by his lacking the proper card to continue an established sequence. One of the earliest Stops games of which we have record was Comet, described by Abbé Bellecour in 1768 as 'the new game'. There is good reason to believe that the invention of the game was inspired by the return, in 1759, of the comet whose advent had been predicted by Edmund Halley fifty years previously. The mild gambling game of Boodle is often played 'for buttons' at social parties.*

PLAYERS. From three to about eight.

CARDS. A regular pack of 52. In each suit the cards rank: A (high), K, Q, J, 10, 9, 8, 7, 6, 5, 4, 3, 2 (low).

LAYOUT. From a second pack are taken the ♥A, ♣K, ♦Q, and ♠J. These four cards, placed in a square in the centre of the table, form the *layout*; they and the corresponding cards of the pack used for play are called *boodle cards*.

CHIPS. All participants are provided at the beginning of a game with equal numbers of poker chips, matchsticks or other tokens. Before each deal, the dealer must place two chips on each boodle card in the layout, and every other player must place one chip on each. (An alternative rule is that each player may distribute his chips as he pleases on the boodle cards in the layout.)

THE DEAL. The right to deal first should be decided by chance. The usual way is for any player to deal cards one at a time until the first jack shows; that player deals first.

The turn to deal passes in rotation to the left (clockwise), and a game is completed when each player has dealt once.

The dealer distributes cards one at a time to his left until the pack is exhausted. Thus, some hands may have one more card than others, but this does not matter. One more hand is dealt than the number of players; this extra hand, the *widow*, is placed at dealer's immediate left.

THE AUCTION. After looking at his hand, dealer may elect to discard it and take the widow instead. If he decides to keep his original hand, he must offer the widow for sale. The others, after looking at their hands, may bid for it in chips, and it goes to the highest bidder, the chips in payment going to the dealer. If no bid is made, the widow is set aside. It may not be seen except by the player who buys it or the dealer if he takes it.

THE PLAY. A play consists of showing a card face up. Cards as played may be thrown into a common pile or may be kept face up in front of their owners.

The opponent on the dealer's left plays first. He may play any suit, but must play the lowest card he holds in that suit. The player having the next-higher card of the same suit must then play it, and so following – the turn to play does not rotate, but passes to whoever can continue the upward sequence in the same suit.

In order to facilitate the play, the leader customarily names the suit and sequence of his card, and the following players call out the ranks they add to it, as, 'Five of hearts', 'Six of hearts'.

The sequence of plays is eventually stopped, either because it reaches the ace or because the next card in sequence is not available (being in the discarded hand or in the previous plays). The last player is then entitled to start a new sequence. He must play his lowest card in the suit he selects and he must choose a new suit; if he has only cards of the old suit, he must pass, and the turn goes to his left.

The play ends as soon as one player gets rid of the last card in his hand. The winner collects from each other player one chip for each card remaining in his hand.

BOODLE CARDS. When a player is able to play a card

matching one of those in the layout, he collects all the chips on that card. It frequently happens that not all four boodle cards are played during a deal. Uncollected chips remain on the boodle cards, swelled by further antes, until finally won.

Irregularities of Boodle

A player who violates a rule of play may not win the deal or collect by playing a boodle card, and must pay each other player one chip; if he goes out first, the others continue play. If the offender fails to play a card next-lower than a boodle card of the same suit, and that boodle card is not played during the deal, the offender must pay the holder of the card the number of chips on it.

The error of leading the same suit is not subject to penalty: it must be corrected, or must stand as regular if the next hand plays before attention is called to the irregularity.

Strategy of Boodle

If you have a boodle card of average high-card strength, keep your hand – don't speculate on the widow. The only time to exchange or bid is when you hold an extraordinary hand of low cards. Even then, there is little to be gained by paying more than about five chips for the widow. As dealer, however, you may gain an advantage by discarding an indifferent hand, for then you will know in advance all the natural stops.

In the play, keep track of the first plays in each suit.

Each is a stop card; e.g. if the ♥7 is a first play, a later lead of lower hearts will surely be stopped at the ♥6. When you gain the lead, first play those cards that are stopped or begin new sequences you can stop, so that you may hold or quickly regain the lead.

BRISCOLA

A popular Italian trick-taking game.

PLAYERS. Two, three, four or six players. If four, play is in two partnerships. If six, play is in two three-player teams.

CARDS. An Italian 40-card pack, which can be made from the standard 52-card deck by removing the eights, nines and tens. (In a three-player game, one two is taken out of the 40-card deck. In a six-player game, all the twos are taken away.) Cards rank as follows: A (high), 3, K, Q, J, 7, 6, 5, 4, 2. Some cards have a point value: A=11, 3=10, K=4, Q=3, J=2. Total value of cards in the deck is 120. The player (or partnership) which scores at least 61 points in a game wins. Games can end in a draw. Play is usually to the best of three or five games.

THE DEAL. Dealer is chosen at random. Each player receives three cards. The remainder of the cards are placed face down to form the *stock*. The top card of the stock is turned face up to define the *Briscola* or trump suit for the game.

PLAY. Player to the left of dealer leads first. A trick is won by the highest card of the suit led, or by the highest trump played. A player does not need to follow suit, *even if able*, but may play any card he wishes. After each trick, each player draws a card from the stock. The winner of the previous trick leads to the next. Once the stock is exhausted, play continues until all the cards have been played.

SCORING. At the end of play, each player counts up the points in the tricks he has won, according to the points noted above.

CASINO

Casino (often misspelt 'Cassino') descends from French gambling games of the fifteenth century. It is now a great favourite among children, but that does not mean it is a childish game. On the contrary, professional card players rate it one of the most difficult to play well and an excellent training school for observation, memory and inference.

PLAYERS. Two. Variants for three and four are described later.

CARDS. A regular pack of 52.

POINT VALUES. The cards are used primarily to represent numbers. An ace represents one; each card from two to ten represents its index value; face cards in effect have no point value, since they may only be paired.

THE DEAL. To begin a deal, the dealer gives two cards to his opponent, two face up on the table and two to himself, then repeats this round, so that each player receives four cards and four are dealt face up on the table. After these hands are played out, the same dealer gives four more cards to each player, two at a time, but none to the table. The new hands are played out, then there is another deal, and so on: six deals exhaust the pack. There is no scoring until the pack has thus been run through. Before the sixth deal, the dealer must say 'Last', since the fact that the pack is now exhausted affects the strategy of play. After the last hands are played out and scored, all cards are gathered and shuffled and the duty of dealing passes to the other player. (Some prefer to play that the previous winner deals.)

THE PLAY. Nondealer always plays first. Each in turn must play one card from his hand. He may simply lay it face up on the table; this is called *trailing*. But he seeks when possible to *take in* cards from the table, or to *build* as a preliminary to taking in. The object of play is to capture cards from the table, in order to score points as follows:

Cards, for 27 or more cards	3
Spades, for seven or more spades	1
Big Casino, the ♦10	2
Little Casino, the ♠2	1
Aces, each counting 1, total	4
Sweeps, each counting	1

(A player makes a *sweep* when he takes all the cards on the table at that time.)

Each player puts all the cards he captures in a single pile, face down, near himself. A sweep is marked by turning one card face up in this pile.

Cards remaining on the table after the last card of the last deal is played go to the player who was last to take in anything. But winning the residue in this way does not count as a sweep.

PAIRING. The simplest way of taking in cards is by pairing. A card from the hand may be used to take another of the same rank on the table. This is the only way in which face cards may be captured: jack with jack, queen with queen, king with king. All other cards may be taken two, three or four at a time; if there are three aces on the table, a player may take them all with the fourth ace.

COMBINING. Two or more cards on the table may be taken by a card from the hand that is equal to their total point value. For example, 6 and 3 on the table may be taken by a 9; or 5, 4 and ace may be taken by a 10. Two or more combinations may be taken with one card; thus 7, 3 and 6, 4 may all be taken by one 10. Further, the card from the hand may capture by pairing and combining simultaneously; 9, 7 and 2 may be taken by a 9.

BUILDING. To build is to lay the card from the hand upon a card or cards on the table, making a combination equal in total to another card in the hand. For example, a player may lay a 7 upon a 2, building 9, provided that he has a 9 in his hand. Having made a build, a player may not trail at his next turn. He must take it in, or duplicate it, or increase it, or leave it temporarily while he takes in other cards.

A build may be duplicated or paired. Suppose that a player holds 10, 6, 3, and that on the table are 10, 4. He may put his 6 on the 4 and add the 10 from the table, as a build of tens. Should his opponent then trail a 7, he could place his 3 on it and add both cards to the build, deferring the capture with his 10.

A player may capture an opponent's build if he has the requisite card. The builder must state the amount of his build. If a player lays a 4 on a 4, he must say 'Building fours' or 'Building eight', and his opponent can take the build only with a card of the named value.

INCREASING A BUILD. A player may increase the total of a build and so change the rank of card requisite for its capture. For example, having in hand 10, 9, 3 and ace, a player puts the 3 on a 6 to build 9; at next turn he may add the ace and change the build to 10. The increase may be made only with a card from the hand; on a build of 6 a player may add an ace from his hand and increase it to 7, but he may not add an ace from his hand plus a 3 from the table and increase it to 10. When finally he (or his opponent) takes in the build, however, he may take with it any matching card or combination on the table.

Obviously, only a build consisting of a single combination (not paired or duplicated) may be increased. If all the foregoing provisions are observed, a player may increase a build whether it was initiated by himself or his opponent, and a build may be increased twice or even more often.

SCORING. After the pack is played out, and so divided between the two opponents, each counts what he has taken in. The total of points to be won is 11, exclusive of sweeps. It is usual to play for a game of 21 points, but among the most serious players the game is either 11 points in two deals or 6 points in one deal and sweeps do not count.

COUNTING OUT. At any time during the play a player may claim that his cards taken in have already brought his score up to 21 or more (or whatever is agreed upon for the game). Play ends and the cards taken in are counted. If the claim is correct, the claimant wins the game forthwith; if it is incorrect, he loses the game.

Irregularities in Casino

MISDEAL. It is a misdeal if the shuffle or cut is omitted and an opponent of the dealer calls attention to the omission before playing any card. In three-hand play, a misdeal loses the right to deal. In two- and four-hand play, either opponent may designate which side shall redeal after a misdeal.

INCORRECT HAND. If the dealer gives an opponent too many cards, that player may *face* the excess on the table and the dealer must play the next round with a short hand. If a hand has too many cards by reason of failure to play in turn, it must trail in each subsequent turn during that round. If a hand has too few cards due to playing more than one card in a turn, it plays on with a short hand. If the stock is found short in the final round of dealing, dealer must play on with a short hand.

EXPOSED CARDS. In two- and three-hand play, a player must trail with a card he exposes prematurely, or with which he tries to take in cards illegally. In partnership play, a card named or exposed except by legal play must be left on the table as though the offender had trailed it; he and his partner may never take it in. None of the foregoing applies, however, to an exposed card that matches a build previously made by the offender.

ILLEGAL PLAY. An illegal play must be corrected on demand made before an opponent plays thereafter.

IMPROPER BUILD. If a player makes a build and cannot take it in (either because he lacks the requisite card or because the build does not fit his announcement), his opponent may add 1 point to his own score or subtract 1 point from the offender's score.

EXAMINING CARDS. Before the end of play, a player may not examine or count the cards he has taken in, except to establish a claim to game. If he violates this rule, the opponent may add 1 point to his own score or subtract 1 point from the offender's score.

Strategy of Casino

In Casino 'all' you have to do is keep track of the cards. Face cards go by pairs, so that if you hold one in the last hand its mate must be either on the table or in your opponent's hand. You surely can keep track of the 'cash points' – aces and casinos. Take a spade in preference to another card when you can, until you have the majority. Try for cards above all else so long as you have a chance. When dealt a cash card, plan how you can possibly save it. If you are dealer, build with it as soon as possible. If you are nondealer, and nothing better offers, save it for your last play since you will have first chance at it next deal.

An example of play:

NONDEALER   ON TABLE   DEALER

34

Nondealer has taken in twenty cards, dealer twenty-two.

Nondealer trails the ♥5. Dealer trails the ♥4. Nondealer puts ♣3 on ♥5, building eight. If dealer should take the build, he would lose the rest of the cards, and nondealer would win the 3 points for cards and the 1 for the ace. Instead, dealer trails with the ♦3. Nondealer takes in his build. Dealer puts the ♦A, ♦3, ♥4 in a build of eight. Nondealer takes the jack. Dealer takes his build plus the last card, making twenty-seven in all. Thus he wins 3 for cards and 1 for the ace — a net difference of 8 points hinging on his third play. (Nondealer cannot play better than he did.)

ROYAL CASINO

This variant is much preferred by children. At the same time, it is regarded by some authorities as superior in its opportunities for skilful play.

The face cards are here given point values: king 13, queen 12, jack 11, and ace is 1 or 14 at the option of the holder. All these cards may enter into building, and may be taken in triples and quadruples as well as in pairs. An optional rule is to count Little Casino as 2 or 15, Big Casino as 10 or 16. All other rules remain unchanged.

DRAW CASINO

This is a variant for two players. The game may be either the original or Royal Casino. There is only one round of dealing; the rest of the pack is left face down on the table as a stock. After playing a card, the player draws the top of the stock, thus maintaining his hand at four cards until the stock is exhausted.

SPADE CASINO

All spades are cash points: the jack counts 2, Little Casino counts 2 as usual, and each other spade counts 1. Game is 61 points and a Cribbage board is often used for scoring.

THREE-HAND CASINO

In three-hand, each plays for himself. Hands of four cards are dealt, with four going to the table only in the first round. Thus the pack is exhausted in four deals. The player on the dealer's left always plays first, and the turn passes to the left. All other rules are as in two-hand. Game is 21 points.

PARTNERSHIP CASINO

Two play against two as partners, the partners sitting opposite each other. Hands of four cards are dealt, with four to the table only in the first round. The pack is thus exhausted in three deals. 'Last' need not be announced. One partner takes in all the cards for his side. There is actually little scope for partnership co-operation in the play, the partners merely pooling their scores. Game is 21 points.

CHAIRMAN

This lively group game has been given a variety of names, some of which are too racy to be printed here!

PLAYERS. The game is best for even numbers from six to eight, but odd-numbered groups may play as well. Players are initially assigned a seat based on a hierarchy from Chairman (highest) down to Office Boy (lowest) in clockwise rotation by any method acceptable to the players. The higher players have a definite advantage in the game, as befits their rank.

CARDS AND DEAL. Two 52-card packs are used; jokers may be included (usually only two). The two packs are shuffled and dealt out completely to the players. (It does not matter if the deal does not come out even.) Rank of the cards is A (high), K, Q, J, 10, 9, 8, 7, 6, 5, 4, 3. 2s are wild, as are jokers if they are included.

EXCHANGE. Before play begins, there is an exchange of cards as follows, depending on the number of players in the game: If there are six or seven players, the lowest-ranked player gives the highest-ranked player his three highest cards; he receives in return three cards of the highest-ranked player's choice. The next-lowest-ranked player exchanges two cards with the next-highest-ranked in the same manner. At the next level one card is exchanged. The lower-seated of the two players exchanging cards must always give away the highest cards he has. If there are eight players, exchange begins with four cards. If there is an uneven number of players, the middle player does not exchange (giving him a slight advantage, because he retains whatever high cards he receives).

PLAY. The dealer leads first and players play in turn, starting from dealer's left. The object of the game is to get rid of all of one's cards. A lead may consist of any number of cards of the same denomination (suits are irrelevant). The next player must play the same number of cards of a higher denomination or pass. A player never has to play to a trick, even when able. 2s will beat any other group of one more card (except jokers); thus, one 2 will beat two of any other denomination, two 2s will beat three, etc. A single joker will beat any combination, including 2s. A trick continues until the last player has played or passed or until a joker has been played. The last player to play takes the trick and those cards are then out of play. (The Office Boy usually collects the tricks.) The player who wins a trick leads to the next trick. If a player has no cards left after playing to a trick, the first player to his left still having cards leads to the next trick. Play continues until all players have played all of their cards.

GAME. The order in which the players empty their hands determines the seating for the next round, i.e. first to finish will become Chairman, and so on down to the last, who becomes Office Boy.

Strategy of Chairman

Though it may not seem so, this is a game in which skill plays an important part. The better player will tend to rise to the top and stay in that area (as in real life). The *order* in which one empties one's hand is crucial. Single cards are generally one's enemy, and in the exchange round it is advisable to get rid of as many low single cards as possible. In play, one should rid one's hand of these single cards, from lowest to highest, as soon as possible. A player should jealously guard wild cards and use them very sparingly and carefully. It is often advisable to pass when one could play in order to avoid breaking combinations. It is generally better to play the lowest available legal card to a trick to rid one's hand of lower cards. When leading, one should usually start with low single cards, unless one knows that one can retain the lead if one leads a different card or combination first. A player should keep careful track of wild cards that have been played.

39

CLOBBER

The name Clobber *is derived from* Klaberjass (*pronounced* klah-*bur-yahss*), *meaning 'jack of clubs' – originally the highest trump card in Central European card games. This popular two-hand development, popular also in France as* Belotte, *was immortalised in American picaresque literature by Damon Runyon and is known by various names and spellings – sometimes even by the name Kalabriás, which actually is a different game, played in Hungary.*

PLAYERS. Two.

CARDS. A pack of 32, consisting of A, K, Q, J, 10, 9, 8, 7 in each suit. From a regular pack of 52 discard all twos to sixes inclusive.

In trumps, the rank is: J (high), 9, A, 10, K, Q, 8, 7. The trump jack is called *jass*, pronounced 'yahss'. The trump 9 is *menel*, pronounced 'muh-*nell*', and the 7 is *dix*, pronounced 'deece'. In each nontrump suit the rank is: A (high), 10, K, Q, J, 9, 8, 7.

THE DEAL. Each player receives six cards, dealt three at a time. The next card of the pack is turned face up and placed partly underneath it. This so-called *trump card* proposes trumps for that deal.

BIDDING. Nondealer declares first, saying *pass* or *take* or *schmeiss* (shmyss). If he passes, dealer may then pass, take, or schmeiss.

If either takes, he accepts the suit of the trump card, thereby becoming the trump *maker*, and play begins forthwith.

The schmeiss is a proposal to abandon the deal; if it is accepted, the cards are thrown in and the next dealer deals; if it is refused, the schmeisser becomes the trump maker at the suit of the turned card.

If both players pass, nondealer may name any other suit as trumps, or may pass. If he passes, dealer has the same options. If both pass a second time, the deal is abandoned.

SERVING. After the trump suit is decided, dealer gives a batch of three more cards to each hand. By custom, he then turns the bottom card of the pack face up. (Thus two cards not in play are known to both players; their identity often affects the strategy of play.)

THE DIX. If the turned card is accepted for trump, either player holding the dix may exchange it for the trump card, thereby obtaining a higher trump. He may not make this exchange after playing to the first trick. (Dealer may delay it until after nondealer has led, but this privilege is often waived as a matter of etiquette.)

SEQUENCES. Three or more cards of the same suit and in sequence have potential scoring value. For the purposes of sequence, all suits rank: A (high), K, Q, J, 10, 9, 8, 7. Sequences of three cards counts 20; four or more count 50.

Only one player is entitled to score for sequence. Therefore nondealer before leading must say 'No sequence' or 'May I lead?' or 'Twenty' or 'Fifty' – announcing the value of his best sequence. Dealer then makes appropriate reply – 'Lead' or 'Good' or 'Not good'. Further information is given, but only to the extent necessary to establish which player has the higher sequence; this player then exposes and scores the sequence; he may also score any additional sequences he holds. His opponent may score none.

A sequence worth 50 is higher than one worth 20; as between two of the same value, the one with the higher top card wins; as between otherwise equal sequences, a trump beats a nontrump sequence; finally, if the players hold equal nontrump sequences, that of nondealer wins.

THE PLAY. The question of sequence being settled, non-dealer makes the opening lead. The hands are played out in tricks. The second player to a trick must follow suit to the lead if able, and, if void of a nontrump led, must trump if able. When a trump is led, he must win if able. A trick is won by the higher trump, if any, or by the higher card of the suit led. The winner of a trick leads to the next.

BELLA. If a player holds the king and queen of trumps, he may score 20 for them by calling 'Bella' on playing the second of the two. The call is not obligatory, and indeed is omitted when this player sees that he is going *bete*.

SCORING. The object of play is to win specific cards rather than tricks as such. But winning the last trick, called *stich* (stish), counts 10.

High cards won in tricks count as follows:

Jass	20	Each king	4
Menel	14	Each queen	3
Each ace	11	Each jack	2
Each ten	10		

At the end of play, each player counts what he has taken in tricks, together with any due score for stich, sequence or bella. If the trump maker has a higher total, each player scores his total. If the totals are equal, only the opponent of the maker scores. If the maker has a lower total, he is bete and his opponent scores the sum of the two totals.

GAME. The player first to reach a total of 500 wins a game.

Irregularities in Clobber

EXPOSED CARD. If a card that would go to nondealer is exposed during the deal, he may accept it or demand a new deal. If dealer exposes a card going to himself, he must accept it.

WRONG NUMBER OF CARDS. If either hand is found incorrect, nondealer – if he has not made his first bid – may decide whether to require a redeal or a rectification. In the latter case, a short hand draws additional cards from the top of the stock; a long hand is placed face down and the opponent draws out the excess cards.

FALSE DECLARATION. If a player asks 'How high?' or otherwise obtains unwarranted information about an adverse sequence when he himself has none or when his is already established as high, or otherwise causes his opponent to disclose facts about his hand that could properly have been withheld, the offender loses the deal. Opponent scores all the points in the deal, including bella.

REVOKE. Failure to follow suit when able, to trump

when able, or to go over a trump lead when able, is a re-voke. A revoke may be corrected without penalty before the next lead; otherwise the offender's opponent scores all the points in the deal, including bella if either player held the K-Q of trumps.

Strategy of Clobber

The normal minimum for a 'take' is a hand containing 40 points in high trumps and side aces and tens. But the state of the score and the particular hand often justifies a take on 35 or even 30.

Length in the trump suit is not essential for a take or a make. More vital is the presence or absence of jass. A singleton jass plus a side ace and ten is the 'classic take', whereas many four-trump hands lacking jass and menel go bete.

Dealer should obviously shade the minimum for a take when nondealer passes, rather than let his opponent name a new suit. But a good defensive hand – general top strength, or several cards in jacks and nines – should seek to let the opponent name the trump.

The schmeiss is a psychological weapon, used with a hand too weak for a sound take but better at the turned suit than any other. Normally, nondealer should not schmeiss on the first round, for then he may be compelled to become trump maker against a 'rockcrusher' in dealer's hand. But this very principle makes the schmeiss in this position a powerful weapon if used sparingly. It can bluff the dealer out of a superior hand.

Never bid in the hope of receiving a specific card in the three served after the bidding. But these cards do add to the strength of the hand (20 points on average), and do justify the expectation that you will receive guards for a singleton menel or ten. That is why such cards are given their face value in the bidding.

CRIBBAGE

Cribbage is believed to have been invented and christened by the English poet Sir John Suckling, who lived 1609–42. Some of its features were taken from an older game, Noddy, of which little is known. Early colonists took Cribbage to America, where it flourishes.

PLAYERS. Two. Adaptation can be made for three or four.

CARDS. A regular pack of 52. The cards rank: K (high), Q, J, 10, 9, 8, 7, 6, 5, 4, 3, 2, A. The suits play little part; the cards are used chiefly as numbers. Each face card represents 10, each ace 1, each other card its index value. Face cards and tens are called 'tenth cards'.

THE DEAL. Each player receives six cards, dealt one at a time.

THE CRIB. From his hand each player selects two cards,

and the four cards are placed face down near the dealer. They form the *crib*, an extra hand that belongs to the dealer.

THE STARTER. After the crib is laid away, the nondealer cuts the rest of the pack, and the dealer turns up the top card of the lower portion. This card is the *starter*. If it is a jack, the dealer *pegs* (scores) 2 points.

THE CRIBBAGE BOARD. Scores accrue so rapidly that a special scoring device is used, a *Cribbage board*. The board is an oblong panel having four rows of thirty holes each, plus some extra *game holes* at one end. Each player uses two pegs, which at the outset are placed in the game holes. Each item of score is marked by jumping the rearward peg ahead of the other by a corresponding number of holes. The pegs are marched away from the head of the board (the end with the game holes) along an outer row of holes, then back along an inner row. The game may be played 'once around', for a total of 61 points, but far more common is 'twice around', for a total of 121.

THE PLAY. In playing his cards, each player retains possession of them, merely exposing them face up in a pile in front of himself.

The nondealer begins by playing any card, announcing its counting value, as 'Ten' if he leads a face card or ten. Dealer then plays a card, announcing the total of the two cards, as 'Seventeen' if he plays a seven. Play continues alternately, the new total being announced each time, until the player in turn is unable to play without carrying the total over thirty-one. He must then say 'Go'. The other pegs for the *go* (as explained below); then the player who called the go must lead again for a new series of plays. The count begins again at zero, and again the total must not be carried beyond thirty-one.

After go is called, the other must play additional cards if he can do so without exceeding thirty-one. Thus the same player may play two or three times in succession. For making exactly thirty-one the player pegs 2; for a go at less than thirty-one he pegs 1. Playing the last card of all (of the eight in play) counts 1 for last, or 2 if it makes thirty-one.

SCORING IN PLAY. Other points may be scored in play beside the go's. These are as follows:

Fifteen. For making the count fifteen, peg 2.

Pairs. For playing a card of same rank as that just played, peg 2. (Pairing goes by rank, e.g. a king with a king, not with a queen, though both have the counting value of 10.) For playing the third card of a rank peg 6, and for playing the fourth peg 12.

Runs. For playing a card that is in sequence of rank with two or more played just previously, peg the number of cards in the *run* (sequence). For example, if the cards played are 4, 6, 5, the last player pegs 3 for run plus 2 for fifteen. The cards need not be played in sequential order to score for run, so long as no foreign cards intervene. For example, if the cards played are 4, K, 6, 5 there is no run.

SHOWING. By *showing* is meant counting and scoring a hand. The hands are shown in strict order: nondealer, dealer's hand, crib.

The starter is treated as a fifth card belonging to each of these three hands. The combinations that score are as follows:

Fifteen. For each combination of cards that total fifteen, score 2. 'Combination' here is meant in the strict sense. Thus, a hand (with starter) of 9, 8, 7, 7, 6 has three combinations of fifteen: 9 and 6, 8 with one 7, 8 with the other 7. A hand of J, 5, 5, 5, 5 has no fewer than eight combinations of fifteen: four of J and 5, four of three 5s. (This hand, when the J also scores as *his nob*, makes 29, the largest possible score.)

Pairs. For a pair, score 2; for three of a kind (called *pair royal* or 'proil'), 6; for four of a kind (*double pair royal*), 12.

Runs. For each combination that makes a run of three or more, peg the number of cards in the run. In the hand 9, 8, 7, 7, 6 there are 8 points for two runs of four, using the 7s in turn.

Flush. For four cards in hand (not crib, and excluding the starter) of the same suit, score 4, or 5 if the starter is also of the same suit. For crib and starter all of the same suit, score 5. (There is no score for a four-flush in the crib.)

His Nob. For a jack in hand, of same suit as the starter, score 1. The jack scored as starter by dealer is called *his heels.*

Proper etiquette is to count aloud, taking the categories in the order given above, and indicating the source of the scores briefly. For example, in scoring K, K, 10, 5, 4, the player would say 'Fifteen two, fifteen four, fifteen six, and a pair makes eight'. The opponent must be given time to verify the score. It is proper to announce the scores for certain combinations *in toto*, as pair royal and double pair royal (call 'Six' or 'Twelve'; do not count the separate pairs). Other standard combinations count as follows for runs and pairs alone (exclusive of fifteens and other items):

> *Double run*, as K, Q, Q, J, scores 8.
> *Double run of four*, as K, Q, Q, J, 10, scores 10.
> *Triple run*, as K, Q, Q, Q, J, scores 15.
> *Quadruple run*, as K, Q, Q, J, J, scores 16.

MUGGINS. If a player overlooks a score to which he is entitled, either in playing or in showing, the opponent may call 'Muggins!' and take the score himself. This rule should be waived when a beginner plays against an experienced player.

GAME. When a player pegs into the game hole that gives him 121 (or 61) points, he wins the game forthwith – nothing more is scored. If the loser has not passed the halfway mark – has not reached 61 in 'twice around' or 31 in 'once around' – he is *lurched* and loses a double game.

Irregularities in Cribbage

NEW DEAL. There must be a new deal by the same dealer if a card is exposed in dealing, or if, before nondealer lays away to the crib, it is found that a wrong number of cards was dealt.

WRONG NUMBER OF CARDS. If a player is found (too late for a new deal) to have an incorrect number of cards in his hand, the opponent may either have the hand corrected or let it stand and peg 2. A short hand is corrected by drawing cards from the stock; a long hand is corrected by discarding cards drawn from it by the opponent. If the crib has the wrong number of cards it must be corrected and nondealer pegs 2.

FAILURE TO PLAY. If a player calls go when able to play, or fails to play when able after opponent calls go, the card or cards he could have played are dead and opponent pegs 2. Dead cards are unplayable; the owner must complete his play with a short hand; but the cards are counted in showing.

ERROR IN SCORING. A player may correct his own error in announcing his score before he has pegged it, but a score once pegged may not be changed except on demand of opponent.

A player may demand correction of an incorrect amount pegged by his opponent, provided that he does so before making his next play, or showing his own hand, or gathering the cards, etc.

Strategy of Cribbage

The choice of cards to give the crib is often easy. Count all the points in the six cards, then lay away the two picked to leave the maximum possible score in the remaining four. But sometimes this course would put points or valuable cards in the crib, so that if the crib is not yours you may do better to deplete your hand somewhat in order to *balk* the crib. Dangerous cards to put in the adverse crib are fives, sevens, and eights, and *near* cards – two in sequence or in sequence-but-one. The best balking cards are very high, very low and *wide* cards generally – separated in rank by two or more.

Sometimes you are forced to split combinations, even when the crib is yours. As a rule, keep a run of three or more, splitting a pair instead, if necessary. Holding a run gives you maximum chance of increasing your count by help of the starter.

In the play, the main principle is to try to prevent your opponent from making fifteen, or a run, unless you can riposte with a score. Obviously, the safest opening lead is a four, because opponent can then neither make fifteen nor pass fifteen and so deprive you of a chance to make it. (He might pair your four – but against pairs there is no defence.)

A card counting ten (ten or face card) is supposed to be a bad lead, but actually is no more dangerous than a seven, eight or any other middle card. In fact, a ten card is a good lead if you have a five: if your opponent makes fifteen, you make a pair. Similarly, a lead from two cards that total fifteen (9 and 6, 7 and 8) is good.

After a lead, the question sometimes arises whether to *play on* or *play off,* that is, play a near card making sequences possible or play a wide card. Naturally you should play on only if you can extend any sequence that your opponent might make.

When no other considerations supervene, play your high cards first, saving low cards to eke out a go.

FAN TAN

There is a Chinese gambling game called Fan Tan, based on guessing the number of beans in a pot. The card game Fan Tan *may have been named for it but is in no way similar to it. The card game – a member of the Stops family (see p. 22) – is sometimes called* Stops *or* Sevens.

PLAYERS. Three to eight; best for four or five.

CARDS. A regular pack of 52. In each suit the cards rank: K (high), Q, J, 10, 9, 8, 7, 6, 5, 4, 3, 2, A.

THE DEAL. All the cards are dealt out, one at a time in

rotation to the left. It does not matter if some players hold one more card than others.

THE POOL. All players receive equal numbers of poker chips at the outset. Before the deal, a pool is formed by antes: one chip from each player with a greater number of cards, two chips from each with a lesser number.

THE PLAY. The player on the left of the dealer has first turn. He must play a seven or pass. Each hand in turn must play if able; if unable, the hand passes and must pay a forfeit of one chip to the pool.

Sevens are always playable. The four sevens are placed in a row in the centre of the table, forming foundations that open the way for other cards. Once a seven is played, the eight and six of the same suit are playable. The eights are placed in a row on one side of the sevens, the sixes in a row on the other side. On these cards additional cards may be played in suit and sequence – upward on the eights to the kings, downward on the sixes to the aces.

THE OBJECT OF PLAY is to get rid of all the cards in the hand. The player first to do so wins the game. Each other player must pay to the pool one chip for each card remaining in his hand; then the winner takes the entire pool.

Irregularities of Fan Tan

If a player passes, and later is found to hold a seven, he must pay 3 chips to the pool and 5 chips each to the holders of the eight and six of that suit. If a player passes and later is found to have had a playable card but not a seven, he must pay 3 chips to the pool.

Strategy of Fan Tan

Given a choice of play, the player should (a) prefer first of all a card from a sequence in his hand, to prepare additional plays for himself; (b) build towards other cards of the same suit in his hand, rather than play a card which is his last in that direction of sequence; (c) choose the card nearest the king or ace, so as to minimise the plays opened to his opponents.

HEARTS

Hearts *is so called because every card of the heart suit counts 'minus' when won in tricks. The object of play is usually the reverse of that in Bridge and other games, where the object is to win certain cards or tricks. Indeed, the eighteenth-century ancestor of Hearts was called* Reverse.

PLAYERS. Three to six; the best game is four-hand. In every case, each plays for himself.

CARDS. A regular pack of 52. With more or less than four players, discard enough low cards (♣2, ♦2, ♣3, ♠2) so that all players have the same number of cards. (Another method is to put any cards remaining after the deal in a separate pile called the *kitty*. The winner of the first trick adds the kitty to his tricks. Some games allow him to look at the kitty, others do not.) In each suit the cards rank: A (high), K, Q, J, 10, 9, 8, 7, 6, 5, 4, 3, 2.

THE DEAL. The whole pack is dealt, one at a time in rotation to the left.

THE PLAY. The player on the left of the dealer leads first. (A common variant is that the player holding the ♣2 makes the opening lead with that card.) A player must follow suit to a lead if able; if unable to follow suit, he may play any card. A trick is won by the highest card played on the suit led. The winner of a trick leads to the next. Some also stipulate that hearts cannot be led until a heart has been discarded on a trick.

SCORING. All players are provided at the outset with equal numbers of chips. Before each deal, equal antes are put into a pool. After the play, if one player alone is *clear* (has taken no heart), he wins the whole pool. If two are clear, they divide the pool. If all four are *painted* (win hearts), or if all the hearts are taken by one player, the pool is a *jack*; that is, it remains on the table to be won later, increased by the subsequent antes.

Irregularities in Hearts

MISDEAL. It is a misdeal if dealer exposes a card, or gives any hand an incorrect number of cards, or otherwise departs from prescribed procedure. A misdeal may be called at any time before the first trick is completed; otherwise the deal stands as regular. On a proper call of misdeal, the cards are thrown in and redealt by the next dealer (the offender thus losing his turn to deal).

INCORRECT HAND. If at any time after the first trick any hand is found to have an incorrect number of cards, this hand must take all the cards remaining in the hands after the last complete trick is played. If two or more hands are incorrect, these excess cards go to all alike, and each faulty hand is charged with the full number of hearts in the excess cards.

PLAY OUT OF TURN. There is no penalty for a lead or play out of turn, but any player who has not yet played to the trick may demand that it be retracted (in which case any other cards subsequently played must also be retracted). If no player (entitled to do so) demands retraction, the out-of-turn play stands as regular. The owner of an out-of-turn card may not retract it except on proper demand of another player.

REVOKE. If a player fails to follow suit when able, he may correct his error without penalty before the trick is turned down and quitted. If a revoke is not corrected in time and is discovered before the deal has been scored, the offender is charged for all the hearts in that deal.

Strategy of Hearts

When the play begins, each hand is intent on avoiding hearts. But once a player has taken a heart, he does not care how many more he may have to take. His only chance at the pool will be to paint every other player or to win all the hearts himself. If two or three are painted, they naturally conspire to paint the others also.

The basis of the play is straight *nullo* – the effort to win no trick, or only harmless tricks. High cards that can be forced to take tricks in three leads of a suit should be played early rather than late. Aces and high cards accompanied by some low cards are not dangerous, but middle cards without low cards are very dangerous. A holding such as Q-9-8 should be led each and every time the opportunity offers, in the effort to dispose of it before cards of this suit are discarded from other hands. A holding such as J-10-9-8-6 is desperately bad and should be discarded whenever opportunity offers, so long as any lower cards of the suit remain unplayed.

Adequately guarded high cards should, however, be saved so long as there is no danger in doing so. Nullo play alone will not suffice if another player has a chance to win all the hearts. A high-card entry sometimes is invaluable in letting a clear hand interrupt a 'take-all' to make a killing lead that paints another hand.

NAPOLEON

Not tonight & Josephine

Napoleon *comes from one of the most ancient and universal families of card games, originally called the* Triumph *family, in which each player holds five cards and the primary object is to win three out of five tricks.*

PLAYERS. From two to six.

CARDS. A regular pack of 52. In each suit the cards rank: A (high), K, Q, J, 10, 9, 8, 7, 6, 5, 4, 3, 2.

THE DEAL. Each player receives five cards, dealt in batches of 3−2 or 2−3. (Dealer must adhere to whichever plan he commences.)

THE BIDDING. Each player in turn to the left of the dealer has one chance to bid or pass. A bid is a number of tricks, from one to five; no suit is mentioned. Each bid must be higher than any previous bid.

THE PLAY. The high bidder makes the opening lead, and the suit of his lead becomes trump. (In other words, the high bidder names his intended trump suit by leading it.) The hands are played out in tricks with rotation to the left (clockwise). A player must follow suit to the lead if able; if unable to follow suit he may play any card. A trick is won by the highest trump in it, or, if it contains no trump, by the highest card played of the suit led. The winner of a trick leads to the next.

SCORING. Settlement is made after each deal in chips or other tokens. If the bidder fails to make his bid, he pays each other player; if he succeeds, he collects from all. Nothing is gained by winning extra tricks beyond what is necessary to make or defeat the bid.

The rate of settlement is usually one unit for each trick bid. But if *nap* (all five tricks) is bid, the bidder collects 10 if he wins but pays only 5 if he loses.

ADDED BIDS. Features often added are the bids of *Wellington* and *Blucher*. Like nap, these are bids to win all five tricks and collect 10 if they succeed. But Wellington pays 10 if it loses, and so overcalls nap, while Blucher pays 20, and so overcalls Wellington.

Irregularities in Napoleon

MISDEAL. If the deal is irregular in any way, the same dealer redeals.

WRONG NUMBER OF CARDS. A player dealt the wrong number of cards may demand correction before declaring; otherwise he must play on with the incorrect hand.

If he is the high bidder (all other hands being correct) he cannot collect if he wins but must pay if he loses. If the bidder's hand is correct and an opponent's incorrect, the bidder does not pay if he loses but collects if he wins.

PLAY OUT OF TURN. There is no penalty against the bidder for a lead or play out of turn, but the error must be corrected if noticed before the trick is gathered. If an opponent leads or plays out of turn, he must pay 3 units to the bidder and he collects nothing if the bid is defeated.

REVOKE. Failure to follow suit when able is a revoke. If a revoke is detected and claimed before settlement for the deal has been made, the cards are thrown in. A revoking bidder then pays as though he had lost. A revoking opponent pays the bidder the full amount he would have won for making the bid, the others paying nothing.

OH HELL

Oh Hell (*politely called* Oh Pshaw *or* Blackout) *first appeared in New York card clubs in the late 1930s. It was said to have come from England, but nothing more is known of its origin. It is one of the best round games for sheer relaxation, yet it is comparable to Hearts in its opportunity for skilful play.*

PLAYERS. From three to seven; best is four-hand, each playing for himself.

CARDS. A regular pack of 52. In each suit the cards rank: A (high), K, Q, J, 10, 9, 8, 7, 6, 5, 4, 3, 2.

THE GAME. A game comprises a fixed number of deals. In the first deal, each player receives one card; in the second deal, two; and so on. In three-hand, there are fifteen deals; in four-hand, thirteen; in five-hand, ten; in six-hand, eight; in seven-hand, seven. The number of deals can be reduced, by agreement, to make the game shorter.

THE DEAL. The turn to deal rotates to the left (clockwise). The dealer distributes cards one at a time clockwise, up to the number per hand due in that deal. He turns the next card of the pack face up on the table; this *turn-up* fixes the trump suit for that deal. The rest of the pack is laid aside and is not used during that deal. In the last deal of a game the trump card is not turned, the hands being played out at no-trump.

THE BIDDING. The player on the dealer's left bids first. Each player in turn must make a bid (he cannot pass); he bids the number of tricks that he will undertake to win. He may bid zero if he pleases, and this bid is sometimes indicated by saying 'Pass'. The size of the bid is of course limited by the number of cards per hand. In the first deal, the only possible bids are one and zero. In the last deal of a four-hand game, the bids may range from zero to thirteen.

THE SCOREKEEPER. One player should be appointed to keep score. The score sheet should be divided into columns (or double columns), one for each player. The scorekeeper must record each bid and must furnish information about the bids on request. During the bidding, any player in his turn may ask how many tricks (total) have been bid before him. During the play, any player in his turn may ask what were the bids made by various players. When the bidding is ended, the scorekeeper should announce whether the deal is overbid, underbid or even (that is, if the total of the bids of all players makes more, less or the same as the number of cards in each hand).

THE PLAY. The player on the left of the dealer makes

the opening lead. The hands are played out in tricks. A hand must follow suit to a lead, if able; if unable to follow suit, the hand may play any card. A trick is won by the highest trump in it, or if it contains no trump, by the highest card played of the suit led. The winner of a trick leads to the next. Each player must keep his tricks segregated so that any other may readily ascertain their number.

SCORING. In Oh Hell a player does not fulfil his bid by winning *more* tricks than he bid. To score, he must win the exact number he bid. He *busts* if he takes either more or less.

After the end of play, the scorekeeper records all due scores in running totals on the score sheet. Each player who busts scores nothing. Each player who makes his bid scores the amount of the bid plus 10. (Some players prefer a different scoring for zero bids: the bidder receives 5 plus the number of tricks in the deal. The theory is that a zero bid is easy to make in the early deals, but becomes progressively harder as the hands grow in size.)

At the end of a game, the player with the highest cumulative score wins.

Irregularities in Oh Hell

IRREGULAR BID. If a player bids out of turn, his bid stands but the turn reverts to the rightful player. If a player bids in proper turn, then attempts to change his bid, the change is allowed only if the next player in turn has not bid.

EXPOSED CARD. If a player exposes a card from his hand, or leads or plays out of turn, he must leave the card face up on the table and play it at his first legal opportunity thereafter.

REVOKE. Failure to follow suit when able is a revoke. A revoke may be corrected before the lead to the next trick, and any cards played to the trick after the revoke may be retracted without penalty. The card retracted by the revoker becomes exposed. If a revoke is not corrected in time, the deal is void; there must be a redeal of the same number of cards by the same dealer, and 10 points are deducted from the score of the offender.

Strategy of Oh Hell

Generally speaking, it is easier to lose than to win tricks. Especially when there are four or more cards in each hand, a player is safer to underbid his hand by one trick than to bid for the full number of tricks he estimates he can win. The dealer has an advantage because he bids last. He should try to make it even if he is doubtful about how many tricks he can win, for then he may get co-operation from other players trying to make the exact number they have bid. The ideal suit has both high and low cards. In the example below, if diamonds are trumps, bid one. If forced to win a club trick, you will not have to take your ace of hearts.

OLD MAID

Although primarily for children, Old Maid *is a simple game that can be enjoyed by adults or the whole family.*

From a regular pack discard one queen. Deal the remaining cards out, one at a time, until all are dealt – they do not have to come out even. Two to eight may play. Each player discards, face up, all his pairs (never three of a kind). Then each player in turn shuffles his hand and offers it face down to his left-hand neighbour, who draws one card, discards a pair if he has drawn one and offers his shuffled hand to his left. Eventually one player must be left with the odd queen and is the 'old maid'.

PALACE

This internationally popular game is also known as Karma. *The object of play is to avoid being the last to get rid of all one's cards. The loser often suffers some penalty determined by the players.*

PLAYERS. Two to six, but best for three or more.

CARDS. The regular pack of 52 cards. With six players, the two jokers are added. Rank of cards is 2, A, K, Q, J, 10, 9, 8, 7, 6, 5, 4, 3, 2 (2s are high and low). To play with jokers see SPECIAL RULES below.

THE DEAL. Select dealer randomly, as by cutting cards. The deal rotates clockwise after each hand. The dealer deals the cards in three rounds: a row of three face-down cards to each player, one at a time; three cards face up to each player, one at a time, covering the face-down cards; a three-card *hand* face down to each player, one at a time. Any cards remaining undealt are placed face down to form a *draw* pile.

EXCHANGE. The players pick up their three-card hand (the last three cards dealt to each) and examine them. Each player may exchange any number of cards from his hand with his *face-up* cards. Players may not look at the first three face-down cards until they are played.

PLAY. The first to play is the player who receives the first 3 dealt face up. If no 3 is face up, the first person to call a 3 in a hand is the first player. If there is no 3 dealt to a hand, then the same procedure is followed for the first 4, and so on, if need be.

The first player begins a *discard pile* on the table, playing face up from his hand any number of cards of the same rank, taking cards from the draw pile to replenish his hand to three cards. Play proceeds clockwise. Each player must either play a card or a set of equal cards face up on top of the discard pile, or pick up the pile. The card or cards played must be equal to or higher in rank than the card(s) previously played. When there are no cards left in the stock, play continues without drawing. If a player in his turn picks up the discard pile rather than discarding to it, the next player starts a new discard pile. As long as a player begins his turn with cards in his hand, he is not allowed in that turn to play from his other cards on the table.

When a player begins his turn with no cards in his hand (because he played them all the previous turn and the draw pile was empty), he may now play from his face-up cards. If he chooses to pick up the discard pile rather than add to it, he first adds one of his face-up cards to the discard before picking it up. He must then in subsequent turns play from his hand until once again his hand is empty at the beginning of his turn.

When a player has played all his face-up cards and his hand is empty, he plays his face-down cards blindly, flipping one card onto the discard pile. If the revealed card is playable, it is played, and play proceeds to the next player. If it is not playable (because it is lower than the previous play), the player must pick up the discard pile, including the turn-up card, and the next player starts a new discard pile. Once again, the player must then in subsequent turns play from his hand until his hand is empty at the beginning of his turn.

SPECIAL RULES. A 2 may be played on any card, and any card may be played on a 2. When a 10 is played to the discard pile, the pile is removed from play and the same player who played the 10 takes another turn, starting a new discard pile. If a player completes a set of four cards of the same rank on the discard pile, either by playing all four cards at once or by equalling previous play, the whole pile is removed from play and the same player begins a new discard pile. When jokers are used (and they must be for the six-player game) they may be played at any time. They are not wild, but force a switch in the rotation of play, so that the person who played the card before the joker must match or beat their own previous play. The new rotation continues until the next joker appears.

GAME. When a player has got rid of all his hand and table cards, he drops out of the game. When he flips his last face-down card, he can only drop out if that card is playable by the rules (i.e. it must be higher than the previous play or be the beginning of a new discard pile). If it is not playable, the player must pick it up along with the discard pile.

The last player left holding cards is the loser and becomes the next dealer.

PATIENCE

Patience *or* Solitaire *games, in their many different forms, probably have a larger following than any other kind of card game. With rare exceptions, a Patience game is a matter of laying out a 'tableau', or original layout; and then, turning up cards from the 'stock', or undealt cards, trying to build up piles of cards which match in rank, colour, suit, etc. On this basic pattern, however, there are countless possible variants. The ones described here are among the most popular.*

Spider is considered by many to be the best of Patience games, for it gives greatest opportunity to overcome the luck of the deal by skilful play. *Chance of winning: 1 in 3 games.*

Shuffle two regular packs together. Deal a row of ten cards face down. Deal three more rows on the first, squared up, making forty cards altogether. Then add one more card on each of the first four piles to the left. Finally, deal a row of ten cards face up on the piles.

This layout is your *tableau* and *foundations* together. The object of manipulation is to get thirteen cards of a suit on top of a pile, ace uppermost, and running in sequence from ace up to king as you go down the pile. Each time you have assembled a suit in this order, you may lift it right off and throw it out of the game. You win if you get all eight suits assembled.

On the tableau piles you may build down, regardless of suit or colour. For example, the ♣7 may be placed on any eight. Of course, when you can, you try to follow suit, but it is more important to get all face-down cards into play as quickly as possible. Each time you clear all the face-up cards off a pile, turn up the next card. If you clear away a pile entirely, you have a space, and that is worth its weight in gold. You may put any available card or group of cards into a space. The only way you can get kings off, other than by assembling complete suits on top of them, is to move them into spaces. But don't be too hasty about doing so, for such spaces are the hardest to

73

recover later. Spaces are needed to interchange cards among tableau piles so as to get suits together.

The top card of a pile is always available to be transferred elsewhere. Also, all cards in proper sequence and same suit as the top card may be moved as a unit. For example, if the top several cards are ♥6, ♣7, ♠8, you may move them only one at a time. But if they are ♥6, ♥7, ♥8, you may move one, two or three together.

Each time your manipulations come to a standstill, deal another row of ten cards face up on the tableau. Before doing so, you must fill all spaces. Then go to it again. After using up the entire pack, and making all the moves you can, that's the end of it – you either win the game or start another.

A sample beginning: the face-up cards in the layout are:

The first thing to do is to build the 'naturals', those that follow suit. You have only one natural play, the ♥Q on the ♥K. The card you turn up is the ♠4. That gives you another natural; put the ♠3 on it. You turn up the ♠A.

Next move any card that can go on either of two others, so that you may later move it again to make way for a natural, should the opportunity arise. Put the ♠J on the ♥Q. Should the ♥J turn up later, you can move the ♠J over to the ♣Q to make way for it.

The ♣8 turns up. Now you have only non-natural plays left. Make a guess, and try the ♠7 on the ♣8. The ♦K turns up and you bemoan your bad luck in guessing! But at least that brings off the ♣Q. Make this move at once, on the general principle of moving higher cards before lower. The ♥7 turns up, at present useless. The remaining play is to move the ♠4–3 onto the ♣5. The ♦9 turns up and now play is at a standstill. Deal another row of cards.

FORTY THIEVES

Forty Thieves is also known as *Napoleon at St Helena*, as it is supposed to have been the pastime with which the emperor beguiled his last exile. *Chance of winning: 1 in 10 games.*

Shuffle two regular packs together and deal a row of ten cards face up. Deal three more rows on the first, making 40 cards in all. Overlap the cards towards yourself so that you can read all the cards. This array is your *tableau.*

The aces are *foundations.* Each time an ace is released, move it into a row beside the tableau. Build up on the aces in suit and sequence until you reach the kings. The game is won if you succeed in getting all the cards on the aces.

You may remove one card at a time from the top of a tableau pile, putting it on a foundation, or in a space, or on another pile if it is of the same suit and next-lower to the card on top of that pile. For example, the ♥5 may be placed only on the ♥6 on another pile. Any time you get a space in the tableau, you may use it to release cards from other piles, rearrange builds, or fill it if and when you please by a card from the hand.

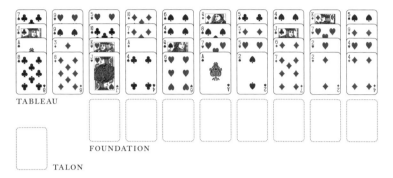

TABLEAU

FOUNDATION

TALON

The sixty-four cards left after the deal are the *hand*. Turn cards up from the hand one by one, going through it only once. Play what cards you can on foundations or tableau. Put the ones not immediately playable in a single *talon*, overlapping so that you can read them. You have to keep track of duplicates, because it is not always advisable to make a move merely because you can. Usually you must plan from the beginning how you are going to make your first space, and this may involve not covering certain tableau cards you will need later.

The top card of the talon may be played off, releasing the next below. In the usual course of events, the talon strings out to great length before you get your first space, and then you have to plan carefully just how to dig back into the covered cards.

As in many other solitaires, kings are a nuisance. Until they can be built on foundations, kings can be moved only to spaces, which are then difficult to recover.

IDIOT'S DELIGHT

Also known as *Aces High* or *Aces Up*. An easy game to play but difficult to win. *Chance of winning: 1 in 10 games.*

There are four *tableau* piles and a discard pile, all of which start out empty. Deal four cards from a regular pack, face up, one onto each tableau pile. If two or more of those cards have the same suit, move the lower-ranked ones onto the discard pile. When you can make no more moves, deal four more cards onto the tableaux such that the previous cards are visible. Only the topmost card of each tableau is available. Continue to move cards to the discard if they match the suit of any higher-ranked available card. If a pile is emptied, you must fill it with an available card from another tableau before you can deal again. Because aces are high, they cannot be discarded. The goal is to complete the game with all other cards discarded, and the aces laid out, one in each tableau.

CANFIELD

Canfield is named after the proprietor of a famous gambling dive at Saratoga. Here one could buy a pack of cards for $50 and play a game of Canfield under the watchful eye of the croupier, then receive $5 back for every card in the *foundation* piles, or $500 if one got all fifty-two cards out. Mathematicians do not attempt to calculate the odds on getting off eleven or more cards, but Mr Canfield found them right and made a fortune. *Chance of winning: 1 in 30 games.*

Shuffle a regular pack and first count off thirteen cards from the top. Place them face up at your left. These cards are the *stock*. The next card of the pack is your first foundation ($5 back already!); put it above and to right of the stock. Then to the right of the stock deal four cards face up, starting your *tableau*.

Whatever the rank of the first foundation, the other three cards of the same rank are also foundations. When (and if!) they become available, put them up beside the first. Build up on the foundations in suit and sequence; the rank in the suit is circular, the ace being above the king and below the two. (For example, if the first foundation were the ♣10 you would build with first the ♣J, then ♣Q, ♣K, ♣A, ♣2 and so on up to the ♣9.) You win the game if you build each foundation up to thirteen cards.

On the tableau you may build down, red on black and black on red. For example, the ♥J can go on either the ♣Q or ♠Q. One card at a time may be moved from the top of a tableau pile, or all may be moved as a unit. In the latter case, the bottom card must of course match correctly with the top card of the pile on which it is placed. For example, a pile ♣8, ♥7, ♠6 may be moved onto a red 9.

On the layout below, move the ♥7 up to the foundation row beside the ♣7. Build the ♣K on the ♥A. Fill the two spaces of the tableau from the stock. Then another space can be made by moving the ♥A and ♣K onto the ♠2.

The thirty-four cards remaining after you have dealt are the *hand*. Turn up cards from the hand in packets of three, placing them in one waste pile, face up. You may play off the top card of the waste pile onto foundations or tableau, thus releasing lower cards one by one. After you have exhausted the hand, pick up the waste pile without shuffling, turn it over, and there is your new hand. You may run through the hand by threes as many times as you wish, until play comes to a standstill.

You are entitled to have four tableau piles. If any pile is cleared away, making a space, fill it with the top card of the stock. After the stock is exhausted, spaces may be filled from the hand. Usually if the game reaches this stage it can be won. The great difficulty is to get all your stock cards into play.

In Mr Canfield's gambling house, you could turn up the cards one at a time and go through them only once; or turn them up three at a time and go through them only three times. It has been estimated that the average was only five or six cards played.

PYRAMID

Chance of winning: 1 in 50 games.

From a regular pack deal 28 cards in seven rows in the form of a triangle to form the *tableau*. Start with one card in the first row, two in the second overlapping the first, and so on, ending with seven cards in the last row.

Turn up cards one at a time from the *hand*, placing those cards which cannot be used face up in a *talon* pile. The top card of the talon, a card just turned up from the hand, and any *uncovered* cards in the tableau are available to be matched.

Two cards match if they total 13, counting aces as 1, jacks as 11, queens as 12, and other cards their face value. Any two available cards that match are removed together

and discarded from play. Kings, counting 13, are removed singly whenever they are released in the tableau or turned up from the hand. You win the game if you clear away all cards of the tableau. There is no redeal.

CLOCK

Chance of winning: 1 in 100 games.

Deal the deck into thirteen piles of four cards each, face down. Traditionally, the piles should be arranged like a clock dial – twelve packets in a circle, the thirteenth in the centre. In any event, the piles must be considered to be numbered from one to thirteen. Turn up the top card of the thirteenth pile (the centre of the clock). Put it face up under the pile of its own number, jack counting as 11, queen as 12, king as 13, ace as 1. For example, if it is the ♣6, put it under the sixth pile, the pile at 'six o'clock'. Turn up the top of the sixth pile and put it under the pile of its own number. Continue in this way, putting a card under a pile and then turning up the top of that pile. If the last face-down card of any pile belongs to that pile, turn next the face-down card of the next pile clockwise around the circle. The game is won if all thirteen piles become changed into fours-of-a-kind. It is lost if the fourth king is turned up before all other piles are completed.

KINGS IN THE CORNERS

PLAYERS. Two or more, best for four players.

CARDS. Standard 52-card pack. Rank of cards is K, Q, J, 10, 9, 8, 7, 6, 5, 4, 3, 2, A (low).

DEAL. The first dealer is chosen at random and the turn passes clockwise after each hand. Deal seven cards to each player. Put the rest of the cards face down in the centre of the table to form the *stock*. Flip four cards face up from the stock, and place them North, East, South and West from the stock pile to start four *foundation* piles. If a king is dealt to any of the original foundation piles, it can be moved to a corner position. The player to the left of dealer will have the benefit of making this move and playing a card from hand to replace the moved king.

PLAY. Players take turns clockwise, starting with the player to dealer's left. At his turn, each player may make any number of the following types of move:

1. Play a card from his hand on one of the foundation piles, by descending order and opposite in colour. The cards should be overlapped so that all can be seen. Nothing can be played on an ace.

2. Place a king to start a new foundation pile in an empty space in one of the four diagonal corners of the tableau (NE, SE, NW, SW).

3. Move an entire foundation pile onto another foundation pile.

4. Place any card from his hand on any of the original (N, E, S, W) foundation piles that have become empty.

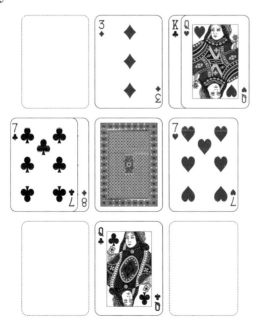

If a player plays all the cards of his hand, he has won. Otherwise, after he has played any cards he can or wishes to, he must draw one card from the stock and his turn ends. If a player is unable to or does not wish to play any cards, he simply draws one card.

If the centre stock runs out, play continues without drawing.

The play ends when someone manages to get rid of all the cards from his hand, or when an impasse is reached where the stock has run out and everyone is unable or unwilling to play any further cards.

SCORING. Each player receives penalty points for the cards left in his hand at the end of play. A king costs 10 points and the other cards cost 1 point each. The game ends when a predetermined number of penalty points has been reached by one player. The winner is the player who has the lowest number of penalty points at this time.

PIG

Pig is a favourite 'ice-breaker' for large parties, whether of children or adults. Any number may play, up to thirteen, and the more, the merrier.

From a regular pack, take the same number of cards from each suit as there are players in the game. For example, with seven players, take the aces, twos, and so on up to sevens, discarding all higher cards. It does not matter what ranks you choose as long as they are the same for all suits.

After shuffling, deal the cards out one at a time, thus giving each player four. The entire play consists in exchanging cards. All players take a card from their hands and place it to the left, then all simultaneously pick up the cards they find on their right. Actually, it is not important to keep these exchanges synchronised.

The 'ice-breaking' feature is that the etiquette of the game permits the player to scream at his right-hand neighbour, 'Hurry up, I'm waiting!'

When any player gets four cards of the same rank into his hand, he must stop passing cards and put a finger to his nose. Each other player, on seeing this act, must quickly stop and put a finger to his nose. The last to perceive that the game is ended is a Pig, and is usually required to pay a forfeit.

PIQUET

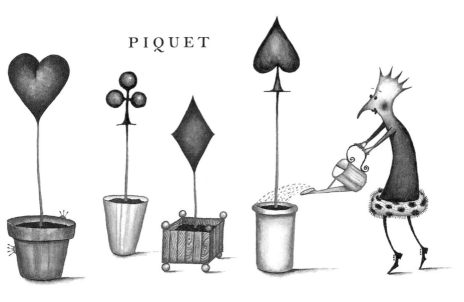

Piquet *was well established by 1535 because it is listed by Rabelais among the games known to Gargantua. There is some question whether the game is of Spanish, rather than French, origin.*

PLAYERS. Two. Traditionally the dealer is known as *major* and the nondealer as *minor*.

CARDS. The pack of 32 (omitting all cards below the 7, the ace being high). The cards in each suit rank A (high), K, Q, J, 10, 9, 8, 7. There is never a trump, and no ranking of suits.

PRELIMINARIES. Cards are drawn and the lower card deals first. If equal cards are drawn, both must draw again.

DEALING. Cards are dealt two at a time, beginning with nondealer. Each player receives twelve cards. The remaining eight cards are spread fanwise face down on the table, forming the *stock*.

DISCARDING. Nondealer begins by discarding any number of cards from one to five. Then he takes an equal number of cards from the top of the stock. If he leaves any of the first five on the stock, he may look at them without showing them to the dealer. Dealer is entitled to take all the cards left in the stock, after first discarding an equal number of cards. He need not take any. If he leaves one or more, he may decide whether they shall be turned face up for both to see or left face down. Each player keeps his discards separate from his opponent's, for he is allowed to look at his own discards during the play.

CARTE BLANCHE. A hand without a face card (king, queen or jack) is *carte blanche*. A player dealt such a hand scores 10 points for it immediately. Nondealer should announce carte blanche on picking up his original hand; but dealer should not make the announcement until nondealer has discarded.

CALLING. After the draw from stock, the hands are compared to decide scores for *point, sequence* and *triplets* or *fours*. The three types of combinations are scored in that order.

Point. Nondealer states the number of cards in his longest suit, as 'Five'. If dealer has no suit as long, he says 'Good', and his opponent scores for point. Having a longer suit, dealer so states and scores. With a suit of the same length, dealer asks 'How much?' Nondealer then computes the pip value of his suit: ace counts 11, each face card 10, each other card its index value. Between suits of equal length, the one of higher pip value scores for point; if pip values are equal neither player scores. The score for point is 1 for each card in the suit.

Sequence. Nondealer announces the number of cards in his longest sequence in the same suit provided that it contains at least three cards. Dealer responds with 'Good', 'Not good', or 'How high?' Between sequences of equal length, the one with the higher top card wins. If the two best sequences are equal in all respects, neither player scores. The score for sequence is: three (*tierce*), 3; four (*quart*), 4; five or more, 10 plus 1 for each card. The player who scores for best sequence may also score for all additional sequences he holds.

Triplets or *fours.* Nondealer announces the number and kind of his highest set of three or four of a kind, provided that the rank is not lower than 10. Any four of a kind is higher than any three of a kind. Between sets with the same number of cards, the higher rank wins. The score for sets is: three of a kind, 3; four of a kind, 14. The player who scores in this class may also score all lower sets which he holds, always provided that the rank is 10 or higher.

Proving. The player who scores for any combination is bound to *prove* it on demand of his opponent. The simplest way to prove a set would be to expose it, but this is rarely done. The custom of the game is for the opponent to demand only the minimum information he needs to calculate, from his own hand and discards, what the precise cards must be. For example, nondealer calls and scores three aces, then also announces three queens; dealer never had a queen, and therefore knows that nondealer must have discarded one; dealer asks, 'Which queen did you discard?' Another example: nondealer calls his point and dealer says 'How much?'; nondealer says 'Thirty-seven'; dealer says 'Thirty-nine' instead of 'Not good', since the other would surely ask for the figure if it were not volunteered.

Sinking. A player need not declare a combination, even when he knows that it is high. Failure to announce a scorable holding is called *sinking* it. The object in sinking is to withhold information that might be valuable to opponent in the play.

THE PLAY. Play begins as soon as all combinations have been announced and scored. Nondealer makes the opening lead. A lead calls upon the opponent to follow suit if able; if unable, they may play any card. A trick is won by the higher card of the suit led. The winner of a trick leads to the next. The objects in play are to score points for leads and plays, as below; to win a majority of the tricks; to win last trick; to win all the tricks. Winning the majority of the tricks counts 10 points. (No count when tricks are divided six and six.) Winner of last trick gets 1 extra point. Winner of all the tricks makes *capot*, worth 40 points (and in this case there is no extra count for last trick or for majority of tricks). A player scores 1 point for each lead of a card higher than 9, and 1 point for each adverse lead won with a card higher than 9. (Modern practice is to dispense with this distinction of rank, counting 1 for every lead and 1 for every adverse lead won.)

Counting. Since scores accumulate fast during the calling and play, each player counts his own score and announces the new total after each new increment.

REPIC AND PIC. If in one deal, *before the opening lead*, a player reaches a score of 30 points or more before his opponent scores a point, he adds 60 for *repic*. Because of repic, points must always be counted in the prescribed order: carte blanche, point, sequence, triplets or fours. If in one deal a player reaches 30 or more *after the opening lead*, before his opponent scores a point, he adds 30 for *pic*.

SCORING. To recapitulate the scoring points:

IN HAND	Carte blanche	10
	point, per card	1
	sequence of three or four	3 or 4
	sequence of five or more	1 per card plus 10
	triplets	3
	fours	14
	repic	60
IN PLAY	lead of 10 or higher	1
	winning adverse lead with 10 or higher	1
	majority of tricks	10
	last trick	1
	capot (includes majority and last)	40
	pic	30

Game is usually fixed at 100, but there are several ways of computing the final result of a game:

Piquet au cent. Formerly this was the almost universal method of scoring. Play continues by alternate deals until one (or both) players reach 100. There is no *counting out* during a deal; the last deal is played out. The higher then wins the difference of the two total scores, but if the loser has failed to reach 50 points this difference is doubled.

Rubicon Piquet. This method has almost entirely supplanted Piquet au cent. A game comprises six deals, so that both players have the advantage of being major three times. If both players reach 100 or more, the higher total wins by the *difference*, plus 100 for game. If either or both fail to reach 100, the loser is *rubiconed*, and the winner scores the sum of the final totals, plus 100 for game.

Irregularities in Piquet

NEW DEAL (by the same dealer). Compulsory if a card is exposed in dealing; at option of nondealer if either player receives the wrong number of cards.

ERRONEOUS DISCARD. If a player discards more or fewer cards than he intended, he may not change his discard after touching the stock. If there are not enough cards available to him in the stock to replace all his discards, he must play with a short hand.

ERRONEOUS DRAW FROM STOCK. If a player draws too many cards from the stock, he may replace the excess if he has not looked at them and if the correct order of the cards is determinable; otherwise the following rules apply. If nondealer draws more than five cards from the stock, he loses the game. If he draws fewer than five he should so announce; if he fails to do so, dealer is entitled to draw all that are left, even should dealer discard three and then touch the stock. If dealer draws any card from the stock before nondealer has made his draw, dealer loses the game.

CONCESSION. Once a player concedes an adverse combination to be good he may not claim a superior one.

FALSE DECLARATION. If a player claims and scores for a combination he does not hold, he may announce his error before playing a card and the scoring in that class is corrected. Should a player play a card before announcing his error, he may not score at all in that deal; his opponent may declare and score all combinations he holds, even if they are inferior, and may score for all tricks he wins in play.

WRONG NUMBER OF CARDS. If, after the opening lead, one hand is found to have an incorrect number of cards, play continues. A hand with too many cards may not score for play in that deal. A hand with too few cards may score for play, but cannot take the last trick. If both hands are incorrect the deal is abandoned and there is a new deal by the same dealer.

Strategy of Piquet

DISCARDING. A player must take into account whether he is dealer or nondealer, what cards the opponent is likely to be holding and the state of the score. Nondealer should discard with an aim to running up as large a score as possible; dealer should be more defensive, retaining short-suit stoppers. A player should consider what combinations his opponent might hold, from the 20 cards not in his own hand, and decide whether to try to beat the likely holding or to offset it by scoring in another category.

PLAY. Much of the play at Piquet can be exactly calculated from information obtained in the calling. The basic principles are the same as in any other game where all or most of the cards are in play: establish long suits by driving out adverse stoppers; save short-suit stoppers to hold the adverse long suit; watch the fall of the cards; lose the lead through adverse top cards that must make in any event, rather than through low stoppers, if you have no long suits to establish.

RÄUBER
SKAT

Skat *was developed prior to 1818 in Altenburg, Germany, out of two pre-existing games, Tarok and Schafkopf. The rules of Skat were codified at a congress of more than a thousand players at Altenburg in 1886. German immigrants brought the game to the United States and an American Skat League was founded in St Louis, Missouri, in 1898. The variant described below,* Räuber Skat, *is simpler than the original game and is gradually displacing it.*

95

PLAYERS. Three. Clockwise from the dealer, they are called: *forehand, middlehand, endhand.* With only three at the table, the dealer is endhand. But four or five often sit at the table, only three playing at a time; dealer gives no cards to himself (and, in five-hand, no cards to the player second from his right), so the active player nearest the dealer's right becomes endhand.

CARDS. A pack of 32: from a regular pack of 52 all ranks from 2 to 6 inclusive are discarded.

The four jacks are always the highest trumps, ranking: ♣J (high), ♠J, ♥J, ♦J. A nontrump suit ranks: A (high), 10, K, Q, 9, 8, 7, and this is also the rank of the trump suit (if any) after the ♦J.

THE DEAL. Each active player receives ten cards, dealt in batches of 3−4−3. After the first round of the deal, two cards are dealt in the centre of the table; these are the *skat* (or *widow*).

BIDDING. After the deal is completed, the players bid for the right to name 'the game' at which it shall be played. This right belongs initially to forehand; it can be taken from him only by a bid that he is unwilling to equal. Middlehand therefore declares first; he may pass or make a bid. If he bids, forehand may pass and relinquish his right, or may say 'I stay' or 'Hold', signifying that he holds his right by making an equal bid. Middlehand may raise his own bid repeatedly in an effort to overcall forehand.

After these two have settled on a survivor, endhand may bid against the survivor in the same way, winning the right only if he bids higher than the other is willing to go.

The player who finally makes or accepts the highest bid is the Player.

A bid names merely a number of points; it must be the possible value of some 'game', but no game or suit is stated in making the bid. The lowest valid bid is 18; the highest practicable bid is around 100, though the scoring value of a game can turn out to be more than 200.

THE 'GAMES'. There are eight possible games, as follows:

GAME	TRUMPS ARE	BASE VALUE
Diamonds	♦	9
Hearts	♥	10
Spades	♠	11
Clubs	♣	12
Grand	Jacks only	20
Reject	Jacks only	10
		ABSOLUTE VALUE
Simple Null	none	23
Open Null	none	24

Trumps. Whenever a suit is named trumps, the four jacks are nevertheless the four top trumps, as stated previously.

Grand. In this game, the jacks are the only trumps.

Reject. This is a game that may be named only by forehand if both other players have passed without a bid. Jacks are trumps; the skat is set aside; the object of play is to take as few points as possible.

97

Null. In both Null games, there are no trumps, and in every suit the rank is: A (high), K, Q, J, 10, 9, 8, 7. The Player makes his game only if he takes not a single trick. In Simple Null his hand is concealed; in Open Null he places it face up on the table for the Opponents to see. The values of the Null games, as stated in the table, are absolute (not subject to multipliers, as explained below).

VALUE OF GAME. The 'value' of a game (other than Null) is its base value, as given above, multiplied by a factor which is the sum of all due 'multipliers'. This factor is at least 2 and can go as high as 14. A player cannot know all the multipliers that will apply until the cards are played out; during the bidding, he can only estimate the probable value of his contemplated game.

THE SKAT AND HANDPLAY. Whoever emerges from the bidding with the right to name the game is now called the Player; the other two, who combine in temporary partnership against him, are called the Opponents.

The Player is entitled to pick up the skat, then name his game. Or, he may elect 'handplay', in which event he puts the skat aside and names his game without looking at it. But if the Player takes the skat, he may not name Null or Reject, in both of which the skat must be set aside.

If the Player picks up the skat, he then discards any two cards. These cards are added to his tricks and count for him in the scoring.

If the Player sets aside the skat, then: at Suit or Grand, the skat goes to the Player after the play; at Reject, it goes to winner of the last trick; at Null, it is ignored.

Having declared a handplay Suit or Grand, the Player may seek to increase the value of his game by declaring 'open'. In this event, he places his hand face up on the table; the base value of his game then becomes 59 (whatever the Suit or Grand named).

PREDICTION. The Player may, before the opening lead, seek to increase the multipliers applicable to his game, by making a prediction (which is in effect a contract): *Schneider*, that he will take at least 91 points in tricks; or *Schwarz*, that he will take all the tricks.

THE PLAY. After the Player has named the game and disposed of the skat, play begins. The opening lead is made invariably by forehand. A hand must follow suit to a lead if able. (At a suit game, the lead of a jack calls for the named suit, which may not be the same as the suit of the jack.) If unable to follow suit, a hand may play any card. A trick is won by the highest trump played, or, if it contains no trump, by the highest card played of the suit led. The winner of a trick leads to the next.

OBJECT OF PLAY. This depends on the game. In Suit or Grand: to win valuable cards in tricks. In Null: to win no trick. In Reject: to take as few points in tricks as possible.

The values of cards taken in tricks are:

Each ace	11
Each ten	10
Each king	4
Each queen	3
Each jack	2

The total of points in the pack is 120.

BID MADE OR LOST. At a Suit or Grand, the Player loses if he fails to fulfil a prediction, or fails (without prediction) to take at least 61 points in tricks. He also loses if he has overbid – that is, if the value of his game (see above) is found finally to be less than his bid (as can happen regardless of what he wins in the play).

MATADORS. At a Suit or Grand, the ♣J and all additional trumps in unbroken sequence with it are called *matadors*. A hand is said to be 'with' so many matadors when it holds the ♣J and 'without' so many matadors when it lacks the ♣J. For example, a hand whose highest trump is the ♦J is 'without three', while a hand holding ♣J, ♥J at top is 'with one' because the ♠J is missing. The number of matadors that the Player is 'with' or 'without' is one of the multipliers affecting the value of his game; it is the most uncertain, since he has to bid without knowledge of what is in the skat.

MULTIPLIERS. The full list of multipliers is given below. The point labelled Automatic is commonly called the 'game point'. Since a Player is bound to be either 'with' or 'without' at least one matador, the minimum total of multipliers is 2.

	MULTIPLIERS
Automatic	1
Matadors (with or without)	*Varies*
Handplay	1
Plus any one applicable item:	
Schneider made, not predicted	1

	MULTIPLIERS
Schwarz made, not predicted	2
Schneider predicted and made	3
Schneider predicted, Schwarz made	4
Schwarz predicted and made	5

SCORING. The Player alone scores, except in Reject. If he makes his bid, he is credited with the full value of his game (which may be far more than his bid). If he fails in a Suit or Grand, he loses the amount of his bid at hand-play, or twice the amount of his bid if he took the skat.

At either Null game, the Player wins or loses the fixed value according to whether he makes or loses in the play.

At Reject, the player who takes the fewest points in tricks scores 10, or 20 if he wins no trick. If two players tie for low, the one who did not take the last trick between them scores the 10. If one player takes all the tricks, he loses 30, the others scoring nothing. If each player takes 40 points, forehand alone scores 10 (being deemed the winner since he named the game).

The score is usually recorded on paper. When a session ends, the average of final totals is determined. (A player can have a minus score.) Then each player pays or collects according to whether his total is above or below the average.

Irregularities in Räuber Skat

MISDEAL. There must be a new deal if a card is *faced* in dealing or if the dealer departs in any way from correct

101

procedure and attention is called to the error before the first bid.

WRONG NUMBER OF CARDS. If after the bidding has begun a hand or the skat is found to have the wrong number of cards, the error must be corrected: a player not involved draws the extra cards from the long hand and gives them to the short hand. A player whose hand was incorrect may not bid. If the error is discovered after the bidding has closed, the Player loses his game if his hand is incorrect, or wins his game if his hand is correct and an Opponent's is not.

LOOKING AT THE SKAT. If a player turns and looks at either skat card when not entitled to do so, he is barred from bidding and penalised 10 points.

WRONG DISCARD. If the Player discards more or less than two cards, then plays to the first trick, he loses his game.

REVOKE AND MISPLAY. If the Player fails to follow suit when able, he loses his game, but either Opponent may instead require the error to be corrected and play to continue (to increase the Player's loss). If an Opponent leads or plays out of turn or revokes, the error must be corrected if possible and the deal played out; in tournament play the *Skatmeister* (director) must rule whether the Player could have made his game without the misplay. (In social play, this matter is settled by agreement, or the players adopt the rule that an Opponent's misplay gives the Player his game automatically.)

Strategy of Räuber Skat

For a trump bid the hand should usually hold at least five trumps. The normal minimum for a handplay bid is eight cards that are trumps, aces and tens. This may be reduced to seven if the player wishes to use the skat. It is unwise to bid in the hope that the skat will furnish a trump or other specific card, but proper to expect the skat to strengthen the hand by one trick. In discarding, the normal policy is to reduce short suits, keeping long suits intact. Sometimes a ten not guarded with the ace must be discarded in order to save it.

The Player should usually lead trumps. By pulling two trumps for one, the Player protects his side cards. He should not overlook the opportunity to discard unwanted cards, instead of trumping, when an Opponent leads a suit of which he is void.

The Opponents should try to keep the Player 'in the middle', that is, throw the lead to the Opponent on the right so that he can lead through the Player. They should watch for chances to *schmier* (discard) aces and tens to each other, to keep them from falling to the Player.

RED DOG

This is a favourite game for social groups who want a betting game in which the action is fast and the demands on brain-work not too great. Though classed as a gambling game, Red Dog *is seldom played for high stakes. It is also called* High-Card Pool.

PLAYERS. Two to ten.

CARDS. A regular pack of 52, ranking A (high), K, Q, J, 10, 9, 8, 7, 6, 5, 4, 3, 2. Poker chips or similar counters are used.

THE DEAL. Five cards are dealt to each player, one at a time, face down. First dealer may be decided in any way and the deal rotates. If more than eight play, each receives only four cards.

THE PLAY. At the start, each player antes one or any other agreed number of chips to form a pool. The object of the game is to beat the top card of the pack (cards remaining undealt) by having a higher-ranking card of the same suit. All bets are made against the pool.

Eldest hand has the first turn. He may bet from one chip up to the number of chips in the pot at the time (the latter is called 'betting the pot'). After he has named his bet and put the proper number of chips in front of him, the dealer turns up the top card of the pack. If the player can show a higher-ranking card of the same suit, he does so and takes back his bet together with the same number of chips from the pot. If the player cannot beat the top of the pack, the chips he bet are added to the pot and he shows his entire hand face up. He then discards his hand, face down, and the turn to bet passes to the player at his left.

A player may pay a forfeit of one chip to the pot instead of betting. Then he discards his hand without showing it.

When there are no more chips in the pot at any time, each player antes again and the game continues. The pot can never have too little to pay off a bet, for the maximum bet is the size of the pot.

Irregularities in Red Dog

A hand with too many cards is dead, but a hand with too few cards may be played. However, the holder of a short hand may discard it without either betting or paying a forfeit.

There is no misdeal.

When, at any time after the deal is completed, the top card of the pack is found to be exposed, it is discarded and the game continues.

A bet paid to the pot in error cannot be corrected. A bet collected from the pot in error may not be corrected after the next player in turn has bet and a card has been turned from the pack for him.

Strategy of Red Dog

Intelligent betting is simply a matter of counting cards to discover whether the chance of winning is better than the chance of losing.

If you are the first bettor, there are forty-seven cards whose location you do not know. The top card of the pack is equally likely to be any one of them. Suppose you hold:

There are three hearts, seven diamonds, and thirteen clubs that you cannot beat. This makes twenty-three cards out of forty-seven, leaving twenty-four cards that you can beat. The odds are 24 to 23 in your favour – practically an even bet.

If you were the second bettor and the first bettor had

bet and lost, holding ♠10, ♥Q, ♣J, 8, 2, and the ♦9 was turned up from the pack, you could eliminate five of the cards that originally you counted as losers – the ♥Q, ♦9, and three clubs. Now there are forty-one unknown cards, of which there are only eighteen you cannot beat (two hearts, six diamonds, ten clubs). The odds are 23 to 18 in your favour.

ROOK

Rook *is a bidding and trick-taking game introduced in 1906 by the toy and game manufacturers, Parker Brothers (now Hasbro) with a special 57-card pack. The cards are still available for purchase. However, this popular game has been modified in various ways to be playable with a standard 52-card deck plus a joker. Two versions are described below.*

PLAYERS. Four, playing in two partnerships.

CARDS. The standard 52-card deck plus one joker. The rank of cards is A, K, Q, J, 10, 9, 8, 7, 6, 5, 4, 3, 2. The joker (the *rook*) functions as the lowest card of the trump suit, below the 2.

DEAL. Each player receives thirteen cards. (In some games, the 2s, 3s and 4s are taken out of the deck; in this case each player receives ten cards.) The last card is placed face down in the centre of the table.

BIDDING. After the cards are dealt, players bid for the right to call trump. Starting with the player to the left of the dealer, each player either makes a bid or passes. A player who passes may not re-enter the bidding. This process continues until three players have passed. The high bidder gets to call trump. A player's bid signifies the minimum number of points that he believes he and his partner will win in the hand. Bidding starts at 70 and increases by 5 each time someone bids again. There are 200 points in a hand, based on the following card values: each A=15, K=10, 10=10, 5=5, the joker (the *rook*)=20. The other cards have no point value.

PASSING. After the bidding round, the winner of the bidding takes the card from the centre and discards a card from his hand, placing it face down in front of him (the card can be the one he took from the centre). The discarded card becomes part of the tricks for the bidder's team and counts along with the trick points. All players now pass three cards face down to their left- or right-hand neighbour; the direction alternating each hand. (Some play that the alternation is among right, left and not passing.) Players must select the cards to pass before picking up the cards passed to them. The winner of the bid may not look at the cards passed to him until trump has been called.

TRUMPS. After the cards have been passed, the winner of the bid names the trump suit. He then picks up the cards passed to him and places them in his hand.

PLAY. The player to the left of dealer leads to the first

109

trick. Players must follow suit if they can; if a player cannot follow suit, he may play any card. The trick is won by highest trump played, or, if no trump is played, by the highest card of the suit led. The partnership winning a trick keeps the cards of the trick. Play continues until all the cards have been played.

SCORING. After play is over, each team counts up the number of points in their pile according to the card values given above. If the partnership of the winning bidder scores fewer points than his bid, they are *set* and must subtract the number of points that they bid. Winning the last trick scores an additional 20 points. Taking all thirteen tricks scores 100 points bonus. Game is usually 1,000 points.

CALL PARTNER ROOK

In this variant, there are no fixed partnerships. When the winning bidder names the trump suit he also calls for a partner by naming a card. Whoever has the called card becomes the partner of the bidder, but his identity is not revealed until the called card is played. The two players play together as a team for that hand only, and the other two players form a team playing against them. At the end of play, each team counts the total value of the cards they have won in tricks. Since the scores are accumulated from deal to deal, each player keeps a separate score. If the bidder's team took at least as many points as the bid, then each member of the bidding team scores the total amount of card points won by the team. If the bidder's team took fewer card points than the bid, they do not score anything for the cards they won; instead they subtract the amount of the bid from their previous score. The members of the nonbidding team always score the total number of points taken by their team, whether the bid was successful or not.

This perennial children's favourite tests their reaction speeds and remains a perfect party game.

For two to eight players. This game can be wild – we don't recommend using your best pack of cards for it!

Deal the cards out one at a time until the pack is completely dealt. It is not important if some players have more cards than others. Each player keeps his cards in a pile face down in front of him. Each in turn, beginning with player to dealer's left, turns up one card from the top of his pile and places it in a common pile in the centre of the table. Whenever a jack is turned, the first player to slap it takes all the cards in the common pile and puts them at the bottom of his pile. The next player begins a new common pile. The object of play is to win all 52 cards.

If a player loses all his stock, he stays in the game until the next jack is turned. If he slaps it first, he continues to play with the cards won; but if he fails, he is out of the game. The last player left in the game is the winner.

The following rules should be *rigorously* enforced (to avoid mayhem!):

1. Cards must be turned up from the stock away from the owner, so that he does not get a peek before the others.

2. Turning cards and slapping must be done with the same hand.

3. When several slap at once – and they always do! – the lowermost hand, nearest to the jack, wins.

4. If a player slaps a card that is not a jack, he must give one card from his pile, face down, to the player of the jack; the penalty card is placed at the bottom of the receiver's pile.

Thirty-one *is the ancestor of Blackjack and can be an ideal gambling game for adult parties.*

PLAYERS. From two to seven, best for four or more.

CARDS. A regular pack of 52. The cards rank A (high), K, Q, J, 10, 9, 8, 7, 6, 5, 4, 3, 2.

THE DEAL. Players draw cards to determine dealer; low card deals. Thereafter, deal passes to the left after each hand. Each player receives three cards, dealt one at a time. The remainder of the pack is placed face down in the middle to form the *stock*, and the top card is turned face up beside it to begin the *discard pile*.

CHIPS. All players begin the game with an equal number of chips (or coins, tokens, etc.).

THE PLAY. The object of the game is to collect cards in one's hand totalling as close to 31 as possible in the same suit. Aces count 11, face cards count 10, and all other cards count their face value. (Some also count a hand which contains three cards of the same rank, scoring 30½ points.)

Starting with the player to dealer's left, each player draws the top card of either the stock or the discard pile and then discards one card from his hand onto the discard pile. Play continues until a player either knocks or draws a blitz.

KNOCKING. At his turn, a player who thinks he has enough points to beat his opponents may *knock*. He signals his intention by rapping on the table, and does not draw any cards. The remaining players then each have one more opportunity to draw (or *stand* without drawing), after which all players show their hands. The lowest hand pays one chip to the pot; if two or more hands share low count, each pays one chip to the pot.

BLITZ. Any player who is dealt or later obtains by draw a hand consisting of the A, K and 10 of the same suit (sometimes called a *blitz*) shows it at the first opportunity in his turn, whereupon each of the other players pays one chip to the pot, and the hand ends. (Some play that any hand totalling 31 points is so handled.)

GAME. When a player has paid all of his chips to the pot, he may continue to play 'on his honour' until he loses again, at which point he is out of the game. The last player remaining in the game wins the pot.

ADDITIONAL RULES. When only two players remain and knocker is tied in points by the other player, if one or both players are on their honour, the hand containing the highest-ranking card among his counting cards wins. If these two cards tie, then the next-highest-ranking card decides. If the hands are identical, then the game is a draw and the two players split the pot, any odd chip going to knocker's opponent.

If the stock is exhausted in the course of play, the top card of the discard pile begins a new discard pile and the remaining cards are turned face down without shuffling to form a new stock, and play continues.

BANKING VERSION. Each player antes one chip to the pot before each round. Dealer deals, one at a time, three cards to each player and three cards face up to the centre (forming the *widow*). Each player at his turn may exchange one card (some allow up to three cards) of his hand with an equal number of cards in the widow, leaving the exchanged cards from his hand face up in their place. If any player is dealt or draws a blitz (see above), he claims the pot immediately. Otherwise, the winner of each hand is decided as above. Winner of each hand takes the pot, there is a new ante, and deal passes to the left.

TOEPEN

Toepen *is often played as a drinking game and remains popular in the Netherlands.*

PLAYERS. Three to eight.

CARDS. A 32-card pack (the cards from 6 to 2 inclusive being discarded), ranked 10 (high), 9, 8, 7, A, K, Q, J (low). The basic object of each hand is to win the last trick.

DEAL AND EXCHANGE. Each player receives four cards. The remainder of the pack is left face down in the middle of the table. Then any player whose hand consists entirely of As, Ks, Qs and Js may discard his hand face downward and deal himself a new one. Indeed, any player may discard his hand in this way. However, any exchange may be challenged by another player. If a player making an exchange is found to have a 10, 9, 8 or 7 in his original hand, the discarder loses one life (but keeps the new hand), while if it was correct, the challenger loses one life.

THE PLAY. Player to dealer's left leads first. Players must follow suit if possible, otherwise they may play any card. A trick is won by the highest card of the suit led, and the winner leads to the next trick. The winner of the fourth and last trick will deal the next hand. Each of the other players loses a life or lives as described below.

KNOCKING. At any time during a hand, once all the players have had an opportunity to pick up their cards, a player may *knock* by rapping on the table sharply. This increases the value of the hand by one life. When a player knocks, the other players may stay in, risking losing an extra life, or may fold, losing the current stake and taking no further part in the hand. A player folds by discarding his hand *immediately* face down on the table. If a player who has no cards left wishes to fold (as a result of a knock in the final round) he calls out 'fold' *immediately*. A player who hesitates has stayed in; it is too late to fold. The last player to knock may not knock again on the same hand, until someone else has knocked. Those who stay in to the end of the hand lose one more life than the total number of knocks. If no one knocks, everyone except the winner of the last trick loses one life; if there was one knock, everyone who stayed in, except for the winner of the last trick, loses two lives; and so on. Those who fold on the first knock immediately lose one life; those who fold on the second knock lose two lives; and so on. If a player knocks and everyone else folds, the player left in wins that hand (losing no life) and deals the next. If the winner of a trick folds after playing the winning card to the trick, but before the following trick has begun, the turn to lead to the next trick passes to the next player to the left who has not yet folded. If the winner of the last trick folds, everyone will lose lives: the winner of the last trick will lose because he folded and all the others still playing will lose because they did not win the last trick. A player may not knock and fold on his own knock.

GAME. Toepen is usually played as a drinking game, but it can also be played with chips. When a player has lost ten lives, he buys a round of drinks (or contributes to the drinks kitty or contributes an agreed number of chips to the pot), the score is wiped clean and the next rubber starts. A player who has already lost nine lives may not knock. Similarly, a player who has already lost eight lives may not make the second knock, one who has already lost seven lives may not make the third knock, etc.

ADDITIONAL RULES FOR THE DRINKING GAME. A player who holds three tens must whistle. A player who holds three jacks may whistle. A player who holds four tens must stand up. A player who holds four jacks may stand up. If a player is obliged to whistle but cannot, he must sing loudly.

GLOSSARY

Ante. A bet or contribution to the pot before the deal.
Auction. The period of bidding.

Bank. Gambling house; dealer in a gambling house.
Bella. In Clobber, the king and queen of trumps.
Bete. Beaten; or, the amount lost by failure to make contract.
Bid. Offer to win a specified number of tricks or points.
Big Casino. The ten of diamonds.
Blitz. A hand in Thirty-one consisting of the A, K and 10 of the same suit.
Boodle Cards. In Stops games, cards on which bets are laid.
Build. Combine two cards to make a numerical or sequential combination fitting the rules of the game.
Bunch. Assemble the cards for a shuffle.
Bust. A worthless hand; also, to reach too high a count, as in Oh Hell.

Carte Blanche. A hand without a face card (it may hold aces).
Cash Points. In Casino, the aces and casinos.
Centre. A part of the layout in Patience games.
Clear. In Hearts, having taken in tricks no counting cards.
Count Out. Score the game-winning points before play is finished.

Crib. In Cribbage, the extra hand formed by the players' discards.

Cut. Divide the pack into two packets and reverse their order.

Deal. Distribute cards to the players; the turn to deal; the period from one deal to the next.

Discard. Lay aside excess cards in exchange for others from the stock or the widow; a discarded card or cards.

Dix. The nine of trumps, when it is the lowest of the suit; the seven of trumps in Clobber.

Draw. Take an additional card; tie.

80 Kings. A meld in Auction Pinochle.

Eldest Hand. The first player to receive cards in the deal.

Face. Put down on table face up.

Face Card. A king, queen, or jack.

Fatten. Play a high-scoring card on (a trick).

Flush. A hand composed all of one suit; also applied to a trump sequence in Auction Pinochle.

Fold. Turn down one's face-up cards to signify dropping; drop out.

Follow Suit. Play a card of the same suit as the card led.

40 Jacks. A meld in Auction Pinochle.

Foundation. The start of a pile of cards in Patience.

Go. Inability to play, in Cribbage.

Go Out. Get rid of all cards in the hand, as in Boodle; reach the cumulative total of points necessary for game; count out.

Grand. A game in Räuber Skat where only jacks are trumps.

Hand. The cards dealt to or held by any player; any player; the period from one deal to another; in Patience, an undealt remainder of the pack.

His Heels. In Cribbage, a jack turned as the starter.

His Nob. In Cribbage, a jack of the same suit as the starter.

Jack. The pool in Hearts, which remains on the table when hearts cards have been taken by each player, or all the hearts have been taken by one player.

Jass. The jack of trumps, in Clobber.

Kitty. A pool of chips belonging to all players equally; also used for widow.

Knock. In Thirty-one, signify a challenge to show hands by rapping on the table; in Toepen, this increases the value of the hand by one life.

Layout. In Patience, the array of cards first dealt out.

Lead. Play the first card to a trick.

Little Casino. The two of spades.

Lurch. In Cribbage, the winning of a game when the opponent has not yet passed the halfway mark.

Maker. The player who decides what the trump suit for the deal shall be.

Marriage. King and queen of a suit.

Matador. A high trump, in Räuber Skat.

Meld. A scoring combination of cards announced or shown.

Menel. The nine of trumps, in Clobber.

Muggins. In Cribbage, the right of a player to take points overlooked by his opponent.

Nap. In Napoleon, a bid to take all five tricks.

Nullo. Play to lose tricks.

100 Aces. A meld of four aces, in Auction Pinochle.

Open. Make the first bet or bid.

Paint. In Hearts, discard a heart on a trick won by another player.

Pass. Decline to bid.

Peg. Score, in Cribbage.

Pic or *Pique.* In Piquet, the winning of 30 points in hand and play before opponent scores a point.

Pip. The symbol ♠, ♥, ♦ or ♣.

Play Off, or *On.* Terms in Cribbage strategy.

Point. The score for the longest or highest holding in a suit, at Piquet.

Reject. One of the games in Räuber Skat.

Renege. Fail to follow suit when able to do so.

Repic or *Repique.* In Piquet, the winning of 30 points in hand, without play, before the opponent scores a point; the bonus of 60 points therefore.

Revoke. Fail to play as required by the rules of the game.

Rook. In Rook, a special card, the equivalent of the joker.

Rubicon. Failure of the loser of a game to reach a certain minimum score, with consequent extra loss.

Run. A sequence in Cribbage.

Schmeiss. A declaration in Clobber.

Schneider. The taking of at least 91 points in tricks in Räuber Skat.

Schwarz. The winning of all the tricks or all the counting cards by one player.

Sequence. Three or more cards of the same suit and consecutive rank.

Shoe. A device used in gambling houses from which cards are dealt.

Shoot the Moon. In Hearts, win all the counting cards.

Shuffle. Mix the cards in the pack preparatory to dealing.

60 Queens. A meld of four queens, in Auction Pinochle.

Smear or *Schmier.* To fatten.

Stand. Accept the trump, or one's hand, as the case may be, without further effort at improvement.

Starter. In Cribbage, the card turned up by dealer prior to play.

Stock. Cards not dealt, but available for future use.

Sweep. In Casino, taking in every card on the table.

Tableau. In Patience, that part of the layout, excluding foundations, on which builds are made.

Talon. Cards laid aside or discarded; also, occasionally, the stock.

Tenth Card. A card counting 10 points.

Trick. One card from the hand of each player.

Trump. A card, or the suit, which is especially privileged to win over cards of other suits.

Trump Card. One turned to fix trumps for the deal after the hands are dealt.

Turn-Up. A card turned face up, especially after the deal, to fix or propose trump.

Wastepile. Talon; a pile of discards; cards laid aside as unwanted or as unplayable.

Widow. A batch of cards dealt separately from the players' hands.

Wild Card. A card which the holder may designate as representing any other card.

GUIDE TO CARD GAMES

Game	Number of Packs needed	Number of Players	Suitable for children
Auction Pinochle	2	3 (4, 5)	
Baccarat Chemin-de-Fer	3+	10+	
Beggar-Your-Neighbour	1	2	✝
Boodle	1	3−8	
Briscola	1	2−6	
Casino	1	2	✝
Royal Casino	1	2	✝
Draw Casino	1	2	✝
Spade Casino	1	2	✝
Three-Hand Casino	1	3	✝
Partnership Casino	1	4	✝
Chairman	2	6−8	
Clobber	1	2	
Cribbage	1	2	
Fan Tan	1	3−8	
Hearts	1	3−6	
Napoleon	1	2−6	
Oh Hell	1	3−7	
Old Maid	1	2−8	✝
Palace	1	2−6	
Patience			
Spider	2	1	
Forty Thieves	2	1	
Idiot's Delight	1	1	
Canfield	1	1	
Pyramid	1	1	
Clock	1	1	
Kings in the Corners	1	2−4	
Pig	1	3−13	✝
Piquet	1	2	
Räuber Skat	1	3	
Red Dog	1	2−10	
Rook	1	4	
Call Partner Rook	1	4	
Slapjack	1	2−8	✝
Thirty-one	1	2−7	
Toepen	1	3−8